OWN YOUR
NICHE

Hype-Free Internet Marketing Tactics
to Establish Authority in Your Field
and Promote Your Service-Based Business

Stephanie Chandler

AUTHORITY
PUBLISHING

OWN YOUR NICHE: Hype-Free Internet Marketing Tactics
to Establish Authority in Your Field and Promote Your Service-Based Business
By Stephanie Chandler

1. BUSINESS & ECONOMICS / E-Commerce / Internet Marketing 2. BUSINESS & ECONOMICS / Entrepreneurship 3. BUSINESS & ECONOMICS / Marketing / General

ISBN: 978-1-935953-28-9

Printed in the United States of America
10 9 8 7 6 5 4 3 2 1

Authority Publishing
11230 Gold Express Dr. #310-413
Gold River, CA 95670
877-800-1097
www.AuthorityPublishing.com

For Ben, my spirited, smart, funny, stubborn son who reminds me every day what really matters in this world. May you always question the rules and follow your heart.

Contents

Introduction
Removing the Hype from Internet Marketing

"Don't be trapped by dogma, which is living with the results of other people's thinking. Don't let the noise of others' opinions drown out the noise of your own inner voice."
—Steve Jobs

This book is going to contradict some of the hype you may have heard about marketing online. If you're looking for guidance on how to write long, manipulative online sales letters, how to coax bigger, badder sales with invasive email marketing strategies, or how you can churn content onto Twitter every five minutes, then this probably isn't the right book for you.

This book won't teach you how to conduct business with a megaphone or command people to pay attention and get out their wallets now because time is running out and the offer is limited and it will make them rich beyond their wildest dreams. That kind of in-your-face marketing doesn't pass the gut test with me, and it's not the only way to promote your business or make money online.

Own Your Niche is about getting visibility with the right audience online and offline in a high-integrity way. It's about checking in with your instincts, questioning the advice you've heard, and communicating with your audience with authenticity, in a way that feels right to you.

It is also about choosing the right audience, demonstrating your authority in your field, showcasing your unique skills, and bringing value to your audience. It's about building loyalty, community, and brand recognition, giving more than receiving, and it's definitely about growing your business.

What every business needs is visibility and loyalty with the right audience. That means that they follow your blog, sign up for your newsletter, engage with you on social media, participate in your programs, devour your content, and gain respect for you and your business. These efforts remove the barrier to purchase without arm-twisting or in-your-face methods. Your prospects will buy from you because you provide value and solutions to their problems—all with authenticity and integrity.

Refusing the Churn-and-Burn

There's a lot of marketing advice out there, and some of it is downright lousy. For years I've been watching marketers use and teach tactics that make me cringe. For example, some marketers treat their email lists like megaphones and will tell you to do the same. I have grown tired of signing up for newsletters only to end up unsubscribing soon after because of the invasive messages that follow.

Recently, I signed up for two different newsletters only to be hammered with *daily* auto-responder messages. One marketer filled his messages with affiliate links and sales offers, which promptly arrived day after day, each message insisting that I could not possibly live without the solution offered. Another filled hers with self-promotional sales ploys and invitations to spend thousands of dollars on her "exclusive" coaching packages.

Sadly, these folks know exactly what they are doing. They know that a high percentage of recipients will unsubscribe. But they don't care because by sheer numbers they will still generate some sales from those who want to believe in what they're selling. They also work aggressively to add new subscribers to their lists on a regular basis. So for every subscriber lost, another is added. And if you sign up for their coaching programs, they will tell you to do the same!

Are these people making big money online? Some are, yes, because of the numbers game and the churn-and-burn strategies they use. It starts with a low-dollar offer followed by offers that climb up the ladder to hundreds, thousands, and even tens of thousands of dollars. They will hate this book, though they are laughing all the way to the bank.

I've also talked with countless people who have paid big money for programs and "blueprints," only to end up struggling because they couldn't get the tactics to work for them. Too often they end up in debt (after being convinced to spend far beyond their means as an investment in their business), frustrated, and with lowered self-esteem. They assume that they are doing something wrong. After all, they were promised that these strategies would work.

The fact is that these tactics *aren't the only way to get exposure for your business or make money online.* Just because someone says it's a good idea doesn't mean that it's a good idea for YOU. This is where you have to check in with yourself and do what feels right to you.

Part of what makes these marketers money is the massive collaboration with others who employ the same tactics. If you look closely you'll see the same people co-promoting each other, churning-and-burning, and not caring about those who they offend because enough people are willing to get out the credit card and take a chance on an over-promised solution.

I was disappointed to learn that one popular author, whose books I have enjoyed, refers to one of his mailing lists as his "repeat offenders list." These are the people who pay big bucks for his programs and those he recommends, and so he continues marketing to them and delivering offers from his peers who pay him handsomely for access to his golden list.

I don't know about you, but the last thing I want to be called is a "repeat offender"—and I certainly don't want to treat my audience that way. When it comes to email, I have had a long-standing policy to avoid sending out "blasts" to my lists. I have been asked by marketers hundreds of times to promote books and programs and events and I turn them down, despite how much affiliate revenue I am offered in return. Am I leaving money on the table? Yep. But more important to me is that I can sleep at night. I respect my audience and have a remarkably low unsubscribe rate as a result. And when I do have something valuable to offer, my audience pays attention. They aren't burned out from constant offers and promotions.

I believe there is a growing movement against these offensive marketing tactics. During a recent speaking engagement I mentioned that I loathe long-form sales letters and refuse to use them. This evoked a surprising, rousing applause from the audience, followed by later conversations with attendees, many of whom told me they simply won't buy from those pages. But once again, the people who use those sales letters—complete with testimonials from their friends with big, bold-red headlines reading "But wait, there's more!"—don't care about the sales they don't capture because there are still plenty of people willing to take a chance.

What I know for sure is that you CAN promote and sell online without the churn-and-burn. Imagine if you were shopping on Amazon.com and each product page was converted into one of those long sales letters. How annoying would that be? Instead, Amazon revolutionized the use of social proof by allowing customers to write legitimate product reviews. There are no sleazy sales tactics here, just the right level of information to help you make an informed buying decision.

Don't get me wrong—we still have to ask for the sale online, and we still have to get exposure with the right audience. We have to have sales pages, email lists, blogs, and social media activity. But this can be accomplished in a high-integrity way.

And so the pages that follow reveal strategies that have worked for me and the many people I interviewed for this book and encountered over the years. Like any advice you receive from anyone about anything, you should take what feels right to you and discard the rest. Not every strategy is right for every business.

Perhaps the best news of all is that you don't have to do it ALL online! You can pick and choose your tactics, roll them out one at a time, and find your own combination of what works best for your business. You don't need to be on every single social network, sending out spammy emails, or dedicating half of your work week to online marketing strategies. There's a better way.

And hopefully at the end of the day, your bank account will be fuller and your client list will grow, while you also sleep well at night knowing you have conducted your business with integrity and authenticity.

My Journey

In 2003 I said farewell to a decade-long career in the Silicon Valley. I decided to take control of my fate and pursue my entrepreneurial goals. I knew that I wanted to write, but since I didn't yet know how to make a living doing that, I chose what I thought was the next best option—I opened a 2,800-square-foot bookstore in Sacramento, California.

I planned to get the business cranking and write novels from the back office, which seems naïve and rather humorous today. I had no idea how those initial plans would change, and how the path before me was about to twist and turn in some incredible ways.

About six weeks after the Open sign was lit, I thought I had made a huge mistake. I didn't want to run a retail business. I hated the daily grind of managing the store and the endless issues that were involved. Dealing with cockroaches in the building from the restaurant next door (eew!), middle-of-the-night security alarm calls, employee challenges, and lugging out the trash just wasn't as romantic as I had imagined.

Add to that the fact that the store was located in a strip mall with no street visibility and foot traffic didn't come easily, and it felt like a colossal challenge. I realized I had to step up my marketing efforts, so I ticked off the tactics in my marketing plan. I bought big, expensive phone book ads, purchased advertising in local papers and coupon mailers, and threw a lot of money at the challenges before me. But the money I spent produced mediocre results and I knew I had to find a better way.

I began studying search engine optimization (SEO) strategies and applying them to the store's website. Within days it moved to the top results on Google, which led to a huge increase in the number of phone calls we received and the number of people who came in to make a purchase.

I started out publishing a printed newsletter and quickly moved to an email-based newsletter. I had to plan ahead whenever sending out an e-newsletter because it always, without fail, made the phone ring and brought customers in the doors. It was like magic and I felt like I had found the key to the kingdom.

I also implemented online sales, which quickly became a significant revenue stream for the store. On weekends we held author events and used the internet to promote them, which was a fun and active time at the store. None of that was due to all that money I spent on traditional advertising methods.

Though I had embarked on the store with a 42-page business plan, it didn't take long to realize that those plans needed to change. And that wasn't the only thing changing. My goal of writing novels was squashed when I realized I lacked the imagination required to craft fiction.

In the midst of all the craziness that came with a growing retail business, I received countless phone calls and visits from my former Silicon Valley co-workers who felt trapped in their jobs and wanted to take a peek into my entrepreneurial world. Their interest sparked something in me. I thought that perhaps I could help them realize that there could be life after corporate America.

And so I took my new-found knowledge of internet marketing strategies and launched BusinessInfoGuide.com, a directory of resources for entrepreneurs. I began filling the site with resources and articles. In fact, I was essentially blogging before I knew what blogging was! And it was working. Traffic grew quickly and before I knew it, *I had an audience.*

Since I wasn't going to be writing fiction, I decided to write the book I wanted to read. I had read dozens of business start-up books, but none had answered all of my questions (like how to negotiate a commercial lease). And so I wrote and self-published my first book: *The Business Startup Checklist and Planning Guide.* I listed it for pre-sale on BusinessInfoGuide.com and it began selling a full two months before it was in print. That's when I really understood the power of the internet and more importantly, the power of building an audience.

All of this was happening while I ran my store. Actually, my staff ran the store; I showed up each week to handle paychecks. I kept the marketing wheels turning from my home office. I was having too much fun with marketing the business website. Soon after, I decided to embark on creating and selling information products including ebooks, special reports, and workbooks. They sold well through the site and inspired my second book, which was published by John Wiley and Sons: *From Entrepreneur to Infopreneur: Make Money with Books, eBooks and Information Products.*

Introduction: Removing the Hype from Internet Marketing

The books led to new opportunities that I hadn't expected. I was getting invitations to speak, inquiries for consulting, and media interviews. Before I knew it I had a whole separate business, which gave me the perfect excuse to sell the bookstore. In retrospect, the store was a stepping stone to get me to a place where I love what I do every day, and for that I will always be grateful.

Since then other books have followed: *The Author's Guide to Building an Online Platform: Leveraging the Internet to Sell More Books* (Quill Driver/Linden Publishing) and *LEAP! 101 Ways to Grow Your Business* (Career Press).

Changes continued to happen as my marketing business morphed into a publishing company. While out speaking to audiences and also hearing from my readers, I realized that there was a great need for a custom publisher to help nonfiction authors produce, distribute, and market books in a professional way. I also knew that a book was the ultimate ticket to establishing authority in your field, and so my company, Authority Publishing, was born.

None of this would have been possible without the internet, which today plays a significant role in everything I do. I have accomplished all of this without a single long-form sales letter. My mission has been to be generous with information, to share valuable content on the internet, and to inspire sales as a result of that work (which never really *feels* like work to me). These efforts and strategies are the foundation of this book. It is the book I wish I'd had to guide me through this journey because it would have saved me a lot of time and frustration.

Here's an email I recently received via LinkedIn:

Hello Stephanie,

Thank you for all the advice you give daily. I have bought your book and learned plenty from your suggestions. I am [a doctor] developing [several books]... I was wondering if your company can help me with the design and editing of my series?... Thank you for your help.

After a phone discussion, this author downloaded more of my books to his Kindle and within a few days decided to hire my company to produce a series of books for him. This is proof that what you're about to read works. He didn't choose us because we offer the lowest prices (we don't) or based on some urgent offer or hyped-up promise. He had followed my work and blog posts online and appreciated the helpful advice he had received. This is how the majority of my clients come to me, and how yours can find you, too.

The strategies in *Own Your Niche* are geared toward service-based businesses including consultants, coaches, speakers, authors, doctors, attorneys, financial professionals, creative professionals, freelancers, and businesses of all sizes that provide a service because you have a unique opportunity to reach a niche audience online with great content.

My hope is that this book will inspire your journey and will help you achieve business growth beyond your wildest dreams.

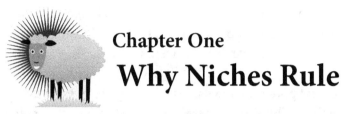

Chapter One
Why Niches Rule

"We owe almost all our knowledge not to those who have agreed, but to those who have differed."
—Charles Caleb Colton

I see a lot of business owners throwing spaghetti at the walls to see what sticks. Their marketing tactics lack focus, and so they try a little of everything and get frustrated when they don't get the results they expect. This is one of the main reasons why so many entrepreneurs dread marketing.

Though marketing does involve testing to figure out what works for your business, there is an important first step that is often missed. *You need to know who you are marketing to*—and that audience should be narrowly defined. Once you do this, it can change everything about the results you get from your efforts.

Choosing a Niche

Everything about marketing comes down to the audience—your target audience. And the audience is different for every business. Once you identify your audience, every marketing decision you make becomes easier because you can gather data to help you find that audience and you can begin building your service offerings and your marketing campaigns around their needs. More importantly, the more narrow your focus, the better chance you have of standing out.

For example, general contractors are often skilled at doing many tasks. It can be tempting to remain a generalist in order to try to get what you perceive to be the most work possible. When a potential client calls and asks for a bathroom remodel, room addition, flooring installation, or garage make-over, the answer is always, "Yes, sure, we can do that!"

There are several potential downsides to saying yes to everything. First of all, you can't possibly be an expert in all areas (unless you employ a large team of specialists in each area). Second, your portfolio of work can appear unfocused. If you said yes to everything and then showed photos of your wide variety of jobs to potential clients, they might think, "Gee, he does a lot, but I only see one example of a bathroom remodel. I wish I could see more examples. I wonder if he really has the right experience to do this job."

On the flip side, if you met with a potential client who wanted her kitchen remodeled and you whipped out a portfolio of photos showing the many dazzling kitchens you created, a bright light would shine around you. You would be the *obvious authority in your field*—a field that is quite crowded with generalists.

Now, you may be thinking that what I'm suggesting sounds crazy because you would be giving up other opportunities and walking away from (gulp!) revenue from other types of jobs. But walking away from that other work frees you up to focus on your target audience: people who want kitchen remodels. And odds will be in your favor that once you narrow your focus and choose a powerful niche, your business will begin to flourish in some incredible ways.

I know a financial advisor who decided to specialize in working with divorced women. This move quickly made her the go-to person for women going through a divorce or already single, yet she still has plenty of non-divorced clients. The point is that her specialty has helped her stand out in a crowded field. And her choice of niche markets is rather large considering the rate of divorce in this country.

Benefits of Choosing a Niche

❖ Stand out against the competition, which are usually generalists

❖ Increase appeal with your niche audience because they will feel confident they are working with an authority who understands their needs

❖ Referral partners will be easier to find because you can work with those who also work within your niche plus those who focus on a complementary niche

❖ You can become the go-to choice for clients who need what you have to offer

❖ You may be able to raise your rates due to your specialty area of focus

How Your Business Can Thrive with a Niche Focus

When your business has a clearly defined niche, not only can you attract even more business from your ideal customers, you can often command higher fees. Sharon Broughton launched her business as a virtual assistant in 2002. She began working as an administrative professional from her home, and in the early years she said yes to most opportunities. But as she developed her skills over time and realized many were advanced skills that her competitors didn't have, she increased her rates and narrowed her focus.

Today, Sharon's specialty is working as an online business manager with clients who use Infusionsoft software (a robust customer relationship tool that few people in her field specialize in). She works with clients who own large online businesses and helps them manage their online activities. In exchange, she commands much higher rates plus a percentage of sales generated. She has also grown her business beyond a party of one and has a team of professionals who work for her.

Recently, during a radio interview, the host asked me if I could go back in time to when I started my business, was there anything that I would do differently. Without hesitation I told him that I would have better defined my niche and my audience. My first business was a bookstore, and it was tempting to try to be all things to all people. At one point we even stocked textbooks, which now seems beyond ridiculous. We could not compete with the textbook stores or keep up with the changing versions of books. We also stocked cheap series romance novels, which quickly proved to be lousy sellers and were hauled off to make room for more profitable categories.

When I eventually sold that store, I took many lessons with me on my entrepreneurial journey. Today, I own Authority Publishing, a custom book publisher, and we have a lot of big-box-style competition. Our corporate conglomerate competitors lead with low prices and publish anything in exchange for a check. I knew from day one that we had to differentiate or we would never make it, and so I chose to focus on publishing non-fiction books. Some people still don't understand this choice. Shouldn't we be willing to publish anything if clients are willing to fork over the fees? But my clients know that their books are in good company. We are selective about the books we produce so we are much more focused on quality versus quantity. This allows us to compete based on quality, service, and a niche focus, which also allows us to charge more than the big "author factories" because we deliver a different level of service.

Examples of Potential Niches

Business	Niches
Chiropractor	Workplace injuries (carpal tunnel), headaches, sports injuries, children, elderly
Nutritionist	Food allergies, weight loss, weight loss for women (or men), vegan living, gluten-free, diabetes
Financial Advisor	Industry-specific, such as doctors, attorneys, or entrepreneurs, single parents, state workers, industry with a high concentration of workers in your area
Website Designer	Industry-specific, such as restaurants or retail sites, professional bloggers, news sites
Consultant	Specific topic-focused, such as leadership for new managers, productivity for call centers, cultivating a remote work force, launching new technologies
Freelance Writer	Articles about health, business, or technology; copywriting for websites; copywriting for healthcare, legal, sports, music; ghostwriting in a specific field

Business	Niches
Graphic Designer	Catalog work, book covers, marketing collateral, book layout, music industry, theater
Life Coach	Women business owners, corporate executives, single parents, people with chronic illness
Professional Speaker	Sales strategies for women, leadership for government offices, team building for tech companies
Holistic Doctor	Allergies, menopause, sports injuries, pain management, fibromyalgia, smoking cessation
Business Attorney	Corporate filings for small businesses, patents, trademarks, mergers and acquisitions
Carpet Cleaner	Families with allergies, apartment complexes, commercial office buildings, neighborhood-specific

How to Identify Your Niche Focus

If you're a selling to businesses (B2), choosing a niche will likely be a matter of targeting a specific industry or people within a specific industry. If you're selling to consumers (B2C), different factors may be involved, such as who can afford your services, how old they are, where they live, or what they do for work or fun.

Choosing the right path for your business is something that takes some careful thought and exploration. Take time to answer the following questions. Consider engaging your staff in this process since they might see things from a different perspective.

1. Are there any specific industries or demographics that we currently serve on a regular basis? If so, what are the future opportunities like there?

2. Do we have a primary service that has special appeal to a certain industry or demographic?

3. Are there specific industries or demographics that sound intriguing? If so, what additional research is required to determine if this track makes sense?

4. What does the competitive landscape look like for the niche we want to focus on? Is the market saturated or is the field wide open?

5. What are our opportunities to make an impact in the chosen niche? What can we do differently from everyone else?

6. Is this niche growing, flat, or on the decline?

Research Your Niche

Before you settle on a niche, it's important to investigate the demand within that niche, the opportunities and risks, plus the competitive landscape. Following are several ways you can research a potential niche.

Conduct Surveys and Interviews

One of the best ways to understand a market is to go right to the source. You can do this by conducting surveys, interviews, or focus groups with your intended audience. Ask important questions about what influences their buying decisions, how much they spend on related services annually, what they like and dislike about competitor solutions, what issues they need solved, and how you can meet their needs. A tool like http://surveymonkey.com makes it easy to collect information online. You may also want to purchase a mailing list or find other ways to reach your intended audience directly.

Look for Industry Data

Use Google to research your target industry or demographic through trade associations and related firms that conduct surveys on market demand. These organizations can help determine if your niche is growing and how much demand there is for related products and services. In addition, check your local library for a copy of the *Encyclopedia of Associations*.

If you have trouble finding what you need online, head on down to your local library and ask a librarian for help. There are all kinds of reference books and databases available free of charge.

Investigate Search Demand

Internet search data allows you to understand the demand for a keyword or phrase. You can interpret this information one of two ways. First, a search term that's extremely popular demonstrates that there is market demand. The downside of this information is that the competitive landscape will likely be greater online because other website owners are also using this data.

A search term with slightly less popularity can still show you there is market demand, but may also be easier to penetrate as the competition will likely be smaller.

Google's free keyword tool is a great place to start: https://adwords.google.com/select/KeywordToolExternal. Type in a search term to find out about its popularity on Google, along with similar key phrases that are related. For example, a search for "life coach" shows 368,000 global monthly searches. This proves that there is great demand for this term and thus, the life coaching industry. However, Google also indicates that this search phrase is "highly competitive," meaning that there are many others vying for traffic from this search phrase.

A search for "life coach health" shows 1,000 global monthly searches, which indicates only a medium level of competition. So if you're a life coach considering the healthy living niche, you can see that market demand exists and the competitive landscape may be easier to penetrate.

Another free tool by Google is http://trends.google.com. Here you can type in a keyword and get a graph of historical data showing how popular that term has been on Google search in recent years. You will also find demographic data showing the cities and countries that most search for the term.

Also check out Google's Insights for Search: http://google.com/insights/search. Here you can discover search trends by location, category, product, or seasonality.

Evaluate the Competition

Understanding your competition is essential to determining whether your business can find a competitive edge in a new market. When I was in software sales in the Silicon Valley, we were urged to study competitors. This helped us position our strengths against their weaknesses, while also allowing us to prepare answers when asked about potential advantages the competitors had.

You can use the internet to find out all kinds of information. Start with your top five to ten competitors. Find out what products and services they offer, how much they charge, and what advantages they might have against you. You can also sign up for their mailing lists or call to inquire about additional details. Don't be shy about this kind of research. You can bet they will be watching you, too.

Additional Resources

http://trendwatching.com – Provides monthly reports on a wide variety of consumer trends.

http://wikipedia.org – The user-generated online encyclopedia may provide some details and stats for specific industries or keyword phrases. Beware, since this is user-generated and data isn't always completely accurate; however, sources are often listed and you may find links to additional research data.

http://pulse.ebay.com – A list of the most popular searches currently conducted on eBay.

http://forrester.com – Provides consumer and business data with technology, IT, and marketing categories.

http://quickfacts.census.gov/qfd/index.html — Find consumer census data by region including state, county, or city.

http://www.census.gov/epcd/www/guide.html — List of census data, including by industry.

http://infoUSA.com – Sells mailing lists, though you can use its search functionality to get insight into the size of your target market.

http://www.marketresearch.com/ — Database of market research reports (fee-based).

http://www.marketingresearch.org/ — Provides market research data and a directory of certified research professionals so that you can find and hire help for conducting market research.

http://www.scip.org/ — Association of Strategic and Competitive Intelligence Professionals, where you can find firms to hire for assistance.

Making the Decision to Shift Your Focus

As you make the transition to focus on a specific niche, know that you don't have to turn away other business completely. If you're worried that narrowing your focus could create a cash crunch, then gradually make the change. Begin to focus your marketing efforts on reaching your newly defined audience while you continue to accept other work. Over time, your marketing should catch up and you will discover how much easier it is to generate business when your target audience is clearly defined and your services align with their needs.

In fact, you might even get to a point where you are too busy with your niche work to even accept other jobs. If this happens, you will need to hire some additional help. Growing pains like this can be a good problem to have, but don't let high demand have an adverse affect on your ability to deliver great service or accept new clients. I've seen too many service providers turn away business because they couldn't keep up with demand, which makes no sense at all to me! Do your best to stay one step ahead of the growth.

Eventually, you may want to develop strategic relationships with companies that provide the services you no longer offer. For example, if you're a consultant who specializes in working with technology companies and you receive an opportunity to work with a retail business, align with someone who works with retailers and who you can confidently recommend. Ideally you will form an alliance so that you can refer business to each other on an ongoing basis.

Develop Your Niche Identity

Once you have identified your niche focus, everything you do must convey that to your new audience. That means changing marketing materials, website content, advertising, and sales scripts. Some companies will need to change their entire brand identity as a result (for those who never really had one to begin with, this will be a powerful exercise in improving your focus).

Using the general contractor as an example, if the focus becomes kitchen remodels, then lettering on the company vehicles needs to be changed and/or added. Assemble a new portfolio for your website and sales calls, along with marketing collateral that explains the benefits of your services along with photos and testimonials.

Identifying Your Unique Difference

Within your niche there will no doubt be competitors in your field (if there aren't, then your niche might be too narrowly defined). In order to really stand out and *Own Your Niche*, you need to understand what sets you apart from the rest. You could consider yourself to be the best in your field, but you need to know how you will convey that to prospective customers.

Consider the success of Zappos, an online shoe retailer. There is no shortage of places to buy shoes, yet Zappos quickly grew into an empire because it was different. The company's inventory is unmatched. You can find shoes from $20 up to $2,000. Zappos also revolutionized service by offering free shipping both ways, removing the risk for buyers. If buyers discover they don't like the shoes, they can ship them back at no charge, no questions asked. This liberal return policy combined with an enormous inventory made Zappos a favorite for shoe lovers everywhere. Without those policies, it simply would have been another online shopping site.

Recently, I met a business attorney who said she specialized in what she called "the usual stuff." During our conversation, she mentioned how much she loves writing contracts. Bingo! She could differentiate her practice by promoting her expertise in contracts. Sure, other attorneys write contracts, but this woman loves them. Her passion and experience with contracts could differentiate her business.

Many of my notes and ideas for this book were kept in a Circa notebook by Levenger. While there are thousands of notebooks available in the world, the difference with the Circa is that the pages are heavier stock and most importantly, removable. I can easily pull out pages and move them to a different section. Because of its unique function (its differentiator), a Circa notebook is more expensive than most.

Incidentally, Levenger (http://levenger.com) as a company is distinctly different in its own right. The company tagline is "Tools for Serious Readers." What you'll find here are high-quality lap desks, pens, book lights, tote bags, and related items. This company could have been just another office supply source, but its focus on its niche market of people who love to read, and its differentiation of unique, high-quality products make it a favorite source for people like me.

For months I've been hearing ads on the radio from a local car dealer that has carved out a niche in serving people with sub-standard credit. The Paul Blanco used car dealership runs ads featuring their "Fresh Start" credit program for buyers with scores below 640. At a time in the economy when automotive dealerships are struggling to survive, the Paul Blanco dealership has found a way to stand out in a very competitive market.

What makes your business different from your competitors? The ability to answer this question in a powerful way can put you on the right track to *Own Your Niche*.

Consider Reputation

People are more likely to tell ten friends about a bad experience than a good one. To get clients talking about your services and recommending them to peers and friends, their experience has to be extraordinary.

Imagine calling a friend to report, "I just had a mediocre burger for lunch at XYZ Diner." Or instead you called to say, "I just had the most amazing burger. We've got to meet at XYZ Diner for lunch next week!" The worst possible scenario, yet the one most likely to take place, is when you call to report, "I had the worst burger at XYZ Diner today. It was over-cooked and the service was terrible. I will never eat there again." And guess what? Neither will your friend.

For many companies, reputation is defined by the customer experience. Consider the cell phone carriers and how they are perceived. Verizon Wireless is known for its exceptional coverage across the U.S. If you want reliable service, Verizon is a top choice. At the same time, the company is also known for being more expensive than many of its competitors. However, because of the company's reputation for quality, higher fees are easier to justify.

Reputation can make or break a business. Reputation can also be cultivated by the business. Verizon's "Can you hear me now?" ad campaign was pure genius. Not only did it become a catch phrase (marketing gold), it set the groundwork for the company's reputation. It was also a bold move. If the company's cell phone coverage was sub-par, this campaign could have fueled a potentially damaging reputation.

I live in Sacramento, and though it's a large metro area, the business community is relatively small and knit tightly together. Reputations here are akin to gossip in a school yard. I could quickly list a dozen businesses that have left a trail of unhappy customers. I could give you an equal list of companies that have earned rave reviews. Our community is not unlike most others. Reputation matters.

While you're developing the new brand positioning for your business, consider reputation and *what you want your company to be known for*. Avoid anything that could highlight your weaknesses—and know that all companies have weaknesses. Focus on drawing out the best in your company.

Positioning Questions

1. Do you currently offer services that generate rave reviews? If not, how could you improve your customer experience?
2. What is unique about your business versus the competition?
3. What do you want your business to be known for?
4. What values do you hold in high importance?
5. Could your values or belief system become part of your brand positioning?

Modeling

In the marketing world, every marketing firm has what is known as a "swipe file." This is where ideas from other businesses are kept, which can include postcards with interesting offers, attention-grabbing sales letters, or smart print advertisements. The point of a swipe file is never to steal ideas, but to learn from others and use the materials for inspiration.

When you transfer this concept to your business, there are a lot of ways you can benefit. By studying your competitors, as well as companies outside of your industry, you can spark new ideas. Take that a step further and you can even ask your competitors for ideas. Sound crazy? Keep reading.

Before opening my bookstore back in 2003, I spent a year writing a business plan and studying everything I could on how to start that business. I also decided to reach out to other bookstore owners around the country. Using the internet, I located contact information and began sending emails introducing myself and asking questions. I was overwhelmed by the responses I received. Because I was located in a different part of the country, I wasn't viewed as a direct competitor. Instead, most store owners seemed honored to be asked for advice. Without a doubt, that effort shortened my learning curve dramatically and set up my business for success from the beginning.

How could you reach out to others who do what you do? What questions would you ask if you had the chance? Why not take that chance and ask?

Study Companies in Your Industry that Are Successful

You don't have to contact competitors to learn from them. You can also sit back and study what they're doing. You can learn a lot simply from visiting websites or reading marketing collateral. Study their services, how they position themselves, and what you like and don't like about how they're doing business. Also pay attention to where they advertise and what kind of media coverage they have received.

When it comes to competitors, I refuse to waste energy worrying about them, though I do try to keep my finger on the pulse of what's going on. It is important to understand their strengths and weaknesses and how they compare with yours so that when you're in a sales call with a prospect, you are prepared to respond to questions about how your company differs.

You can also draw inspiration from businesses outside of your industry. For example, loyalty programs work well with many retail businesses. How could you use something like that in your business?

Become a student of life and pay attention to how other companies operate, and then figure out how to apply those lessons to your own business.

Entrepreneur Interview
Name: Anita Campbell

Business name: Small Business Trends, LLC

Website URL: http://smallbiztrends.com, http://bizsugar.com
(another of my key sites)

Social media links:

http://twitter.com/smallbiztrends
http://twitter.com/bizsugar
http://www.facebook.com/smallbusinesstrends
http://www.facebook.com/bizsugar

Tell us about your business and what you do:

I own a web publishing business called Small Business Trends, LLC. We publish information, tips, news, and advice for small businesses. Think of it as similar to *Inc. Magazine*, except it's all online instead of in print. People often ask, "What is your business model?" It's simple, really. We publish information that we provide mostly for free to our readers. Advertisers and sponsors pay to be visible to the audience we've amassed. That publishing model has been out there for centuries – we've just translated it to alternative media such as blogs and social media, instead of printed magazines and newspapers.

We also have an internet radio podcast that features interviews. And just like many traditional magazines, we have branched out into events. We produce online/in-person events such as the Small Business Influencer Awards and the Small Business Book Awards. And we have a social media website that enables small businesses to promote their websites and blog posts for free.

Who is your target audience?

Our target audience is exclusively small-business people and entrepreneurs. We define small business as a business having 100 or fewer employees. The typical reader is a small-business owner or manager.

Our sweet spot is the established small business that's been around for at least a few years, with a small number of employees (fewer than 20 employees). A smaller group of readers are also sole proprietors and individual entrepreneurs. Another segment is startups, but that's not our main focus. We don't focus too much on the "wannabe business owner." There are numerous sites out there that will show you how to get a business started from a clean sheet of paper. Our advice and information tends to assume that you've already started your business, been around for a little while—such as a year or so—and want to know what you should do to grow your existing business.

How did you get started in your business?

It is not what I set out to do – it started a bit by accident. I left the corporate world where I had been an executive in a technology company. I started doing some consulting, mostly for friends and colleagues, helping them with their business plans, business models, strategy, and marketing. I decided to start an email newsletter to market my consulting services, but I needed an easier online method to publish articles I was writing for the newsletter (using Dreamweaver software to post articles online is NOT one of my skills!).

Someone suggested I start a blog as an easy way to publish articles online. So I went over to blogger.com – and the rest is history! Before I knew it, more people were reading the blog than the newsletter. At that point, I decided to put more attention on the blog. After all, when something does well, you adjust and put more resources toward it.

Eventually, that blog became much, much bigger, and evolved to become my business's main revenue generator (not just a marketing tool). That initial blog grew to become my company's flagship website, with 250+ contributors, daily news features, and hundreds of thousands of targeted visitors each month.

Along the way, we acquired other sites (such as bizsugar.com, our social media site). We also started other initiatives, such as the awards events I mentioned.

What are some of the best tactics you have used to build your audience and establish your authority online?

There are really four "umbrella" elements:

(1) **Produce a lot of content** – This includes writing on blogs. And today you have to not only have your own blog—so that you can publish whatever you want, whenever you want to—but you must also guest post on other blogs. Guest blogging has been a key visibility tactic during 2011, and I expect that to continue in 2012 and for the foreseeable future. You also should submit articles to newspapers and magazines that accept them.

Don't limit it just to text. Think multiple media, too – videos, infographics, podcasts, and other formats. Today, a tremendous amount of your online visibility is tied to having good content that gets indexed in search engines like Google and Bing, and can be found by those searching for what you have to offer.

Of course, producing a lot of content is also a way to establish yourself as a thought leader. So the quality of your content is important. With it being so easy for people to get published online today, you have a lot of competition! Develop a particular angle or "voice" that is uniquely yours so that you stand out. Or bring forth some hard-to-find information that no one else has. That sort of uniqueness is what separates ordinary content from those who get quoted as experts.

Quantity is just as important. Establish a regular editorial content plan identifying how frequently you will produce and publish content online, what type(s) of content, on which websites, and the specific topics that you want your professional name and/or business name associated with. Hire a freelance blogger or writer if writing is laborious for you – everyone needs a little help!

(2) **Engage in social media** – The second element of building your audience is to reach out via social media. Social media amplifies your message – it helps spread your blog posts and videos and other content. It also helps you build a network of connections. And it keeps your name in the limelight. We've found Twitter, Facebook, LinkedIn, BizSugar, and blogs to be the best for our audience. But find out where your target audience spends time. That may be relatively easy, or it may take some digging and experimentation. And focus on a few. Don't be a dilettante – be a dominatrix! In other words, become a power-user of one, two, or at most three social sites. Don't do a dozen poorly.

(3) **Develop a good SEO plan** – The third element of building your audience is to understand how search engines work, and how to get good visibility via organic search results. Remember, search engine optimization (SEO) consists of more than just Twitter and blogs. Your pages must be friendly to search engines; you have to have inbound links to various pages in your site; you will want good title tags, etc. – in short, you must focus on a variety of technical elements that make up good search engine optimization.

(4) **Don't ignore PR** – Public relations is the fourth key to build your audience. PR can consist of monitoring/replying to HARO pitches so you can get quoted in mainstream media, holding giveaways, speaking at seminars, sponsoring charitable events, distributing press releases, and reaching out individually to journalists. Find opportunities to put yourself and other key members of your organization out in the public eye. You establish brand familiarity and thought leadership, and become more memorable that way.

How has social media impacted your business? Any success stories you can share?

We produced the Small Business Influencer Awards in 2011. We had zero marketing budget, except for our time. We were able to publicize the Awards almost completely through Twitter by tweeting about the nominations using a specific hashtag, and holding two Twitter chats and two Twitter-based giveaways. And we put tweet buttons on the site to make it easy for others to retweet when they nominated or voted for someone. In the space of a few months, we had more than 10,000 tweets about the Awards. We got almost 400,000 visitors to the Awards site, and 125,000 votes from the community. And I attribute it mostly to Twitter.

Do you engage in any communities and if so, how has that impacted your business?

I and my team are active on Twitter, Facebook, and LinkedIn. We are also very active on the social media site I own, bizsugar.com, and the community we run at Small Business Trends. I personally participate as a moderator at the private seobook.com forums. I've also participated on some advice sites such as business.com Answers and Quora.

Small Business Trends, Twitter, BizSugar, and the SEOBook forums have led to a number of deeper business relationships, including being featured in books, interviews of all kinds, and even revenue-generating partnerships and business deals.

What role does content play in your marketing strategy?

Content is crucial to the business – in fact, content is at the center of our business. But it's not the ONLY thing.

We learned a long time ago that we couldn't just publish. In other words, you cannot have the mentality of "publish and they will come." That's a quick way to fade away into obscurity today. Only about 50% of our effort is spent on publishing activities. The other 50% is spent actively marketing our content through newsletters, RSS distribution channels, partners, SEO, event marketing, and most importantly, various social media outposts and mini-communities we've created. We have a higher-than-average marketing expense budget (for a business of similar size). A significant portion of our people, time, and money resources are spent on marketing activities.

What advice would you offer to readers who want to promote their business online?

(1) Get good at writing or find a good freelancer you can rely on.

(2) Understand what your competitors are doing. Follow them on Twitter and Facebook, and see where they are speaking, guest posting, or getting visibility. That will tell you who to approach to get visibility for yourself or others in your organization.

(3) Have a solid social media strategy and execute it! Keep your ear to the ground on which social media sites are hot in your industry or among your customers. Make sure your business has a presence there. Develop some internal expertise in a few key social media sites – and make social media a priority, not an afterthought. It will be worth it.

If you were starting your business over today, is there anything you would do differently?

I would have hired a full-time software developer earlier. Technology helps you realize your dreams – and your business model. While there are a lot of do-it-yourself tools, you can accomplish so much more so quickly with custom software. It's worth it.

Quick Tip

Have you ever noticed how some people who comment on blogs have a photo in their profile, while others don't? If you want your photo to appear online, register a free account with http://en.gravatar.com/.

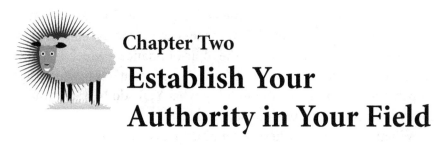

Chapter Two
Establish Your Authority in Your Field

"If you have knowledge, let others light their candles at it."
—Margaret Fuller

Marketing your business with authority is about building recognition in your industry, generating buzz online, and showcasing your company's talents and skills to generate demand for your services. It is about delivering your best content and killer customer service with integrity and passion, while listening to your target audience and engaging with them authentically.

In a nutshell, Authority rules.

Marketing with authority is about creating excellence in what you do and allowing that to shine through. Consumers want to buy from the best and when you establish your authority in your field, you are perceived as the best.

We see authorities in the media every day because the media loves experts. If you watch the *Today* show or *Good Morning America*, you'll see real estate experts, doctors, therapists, nutritionists, parenting experts, consultants, attorneys, and chefs. Many of these guest experts have become media favorites: Martha Stewart, Rachael Ray, Curtis Stone, Barbara Corcoran, and Dr. Oz. But none of these people were born in the eyes of the media; they all started by choosing a niche and showcasing their authority in their respective fields.

Another important point is that many people can play in the same sandbox. For example, there are dozens of financial experts out there:

Suze Orman, Jean Chatzky, Carmen Wong Ulrich, David Bach, Jim Cramer, and the list goes on. What makes each authority stand out is his or her unique perspective on the topic of finance—which is really the essence of marketing with authority. It's not about doing what your competitors are doing. It's about doing what YOU do best, and that's when your light begins to shine its brightest.

Whether you are marketing your business locally or globally, you have the opportunity to demonstrate your authority in your field and use that to your advantage. You can become the best personal injury attorney in Sarasota, the leading life coach in Chicago, or the top financial advisor in San Diego. And thanks to the internet, you can expand your reach online. Stand out from the competition by finding your own unique voice and sharing your personal perspective on matters of interest to your target audience. All of this leads to owning your niche.

How Authority Works

One big company that has done a great job of demonstrating its authority with its target audience is American Express. Over at http://openforum. com you will find articles and resources to help you grow your business. Many of the articles are written by industry experts (authorities!), though in summer 2011 Am Ex began inviting members to contribute to the site. The result is an active website full of resources that attract American Express' target customers: small-business owners.

There's another lesson you can learn from this big company. If you don't have the right expertise in-house, you can bring in experts from outside sources. Content can come from paid writers, staff, spokespeople, alliance partners, volunteer contributors, or even your customers.

I took a similar approach with BusinessInfoGuide.com. After years of being the sole producer of content, I opened it up to guest posts and interviews with authors and entrepreneurs. This move allowed me to expand the site, continue adding value for site visitors, give exposure to deserving authors and entrepreneurs, increase website traffic, and ultimately gain more visibility with my target audience in the process.

One of the smartest authorities I know is Karl Palachuk. Karl is a consultant to IT consultants—he teaches them how to run their businesses, migrate data, and all the other techy stuff involved in his industry. He has made millions by demonstrating his authority. In the early years, he spent a lot of time in technology forums sharing his advice and building a rapport with his target audience. Over time, those efforts evolved into a series of books, podcasts, webinars, e-newsletters, profitable seminars held around the globe, and a popular blog: http://smallbizthoughts.com.

Though Karl gives away plenty of free information, he also monetizes his efforts at every turn. His blog contains a variety of advertisements, he has printed catalogs of his own products and sold advertising within the catalogs, and he regularly fills auditoriums with paid attendees who also scoop up product bundles at the back of the room. In fact, one of his best-selling products is a data migration workbook that costs a whopping $300, which his audience eagerly buys because they trust him as a source who provides valuable information.

While Karl could have run his business like many do, acquiring one client at a time, he instead chose to become a leading authority in his niche. If you're outside of the IT industry you have probably never heard of him, but IT insiders buy his products and services because he consistently demonstrates his authority in his field in a high-integrity way.

How to Claim Your Authority

Whatever it is that you do, it's time to step up and take ownership. If you're a dog trainer, you need to be the best damn dog trainer around. If you're a consultant who works with family businesses, you need to be at the top of your game, which means continuously learning about trends and ways that you can address them with your clients.

I firmly believe that if you're going to do something, you need to do whatever it takes to do it to the best of your ability. That means continually learning, studying your industry, reading books and trade publications, attending industry events, and improving your service offerings. This is a lifelong process.

You also need to get comfortable with being in the position of authority in your field. Some people struggle with the idea of being in the spotlight. But this is not a matter of being boastful or arrogant. It's simply about stepping into your power and letting your light shine.

Take pride in your own talents and abilities and *know that you are in service when you are teaching others.* There is no megaphone required! By simply doing what you do best and sharing it with the world, your authority will shine through.

Following are several ways to get you moving in the right direction. We will expand on many of these topics throughout the book, but here's a primer to get you started.

Start a Blog

If you could choose just one tactic from this book to boost your business, I would strongly recommend blogging. Adding a blog to your website has dozens of advantages. It gives you a place to showcase your expertise, provide helpful content to your target audience, engage with your visitors through comments, and dazzle prospective customers.

For example, if you're an acupuncturist and you write blog posts on how acupuncture helps with allergies or sciatica or fertility, imagine the reaction from a prospective client who lands on your site and discovers all of the helpful resources you've shared. You would clearly demonstrate your authority on the subject matter, which would inspire site visitors to schedule an appointment with you.

Also, when you update your blog on a regular basis (ideally two or more times per week), you will be rewarded with increased site traffic. Google gives higher priority to sites that update content frequently. More importantly, the more content you add to your site, the more reasons you give Google to find you. This was a phenomenon I discovered as I added more and more resources to BusinessInfoGuide. com. Each new article brought new traffic as a result of various topics coming up in Google searches.

For me personally, my blog has brought me countless opportunities, including media interviews, corporate sponsorships, and new clients. We will discuss blogging in greater detail later in this book, but for now know that I believe it's one of the most powerful marketing tools you can implement for your business.

Share Content via Social Media

While studies show that the vast majority of businesses are wasting their time with social media, the good news is that when you do it right, it can be a powerful way to demonstrate your authority, reach your niche audience, attract clients, and drive more traffic back to your site.

You also have an opportunity to stand out above the "noise" that is happening in social media land. Nobody cares what's on your dinner menu, which kid needs a ride to band practice, or that you have a blister on your toe (and please, for the love of all things good, don't share a photo of the blister—eew!). That's not what social media is about at all.

Facebook, Twitter, and LinkedIn each provide a launch pad for demonstrating your authority. You can do this by sharing great content that appeals to your target audience. That can include links to your recent blog posts, helpful tips, articles from other websites, and much more. Despite what you may have heard, social media isn't just about having a conversation with your audience. It's a platform for educating and engaging your audience with smart content.

Engage on Other Blogs

Search for blogs that reach your target audience and get involved. When you post a comment on another blog, you have a chance to get visibility with that blog's readers. I posted a comment on a *Wall Street Journal* article about publishing and received more than 100 visits to my website as a result. It took an extra two minutes for me to make this effort and it went a long way in raising visibility for my business.

When you post a comment, many blogs also include a link back to your website, which can not only bring traffic from other blog readers but can improve your own website's position on Google (incoming links are great for search engine optimization, especially from high-traffic websites and sites in a similar industry).

The key to writing a great comment is to contribute to the topic at hand. So if you've just read a blog post on 10 ways to bathe a cat, add a comment with one or two more suggestions. Or share your own personal cat bathing adventures! Avoid simply saying, "Great post, thanks." Instead, take advantage of the opportunity to showcase your authority in the subject matter.

To find blogs that reach your target audience, you can search Google for key phrases plus the word "blog," or search a blog directory such as Technorati.com. Begin following the RSS feeds for these blogs (get a free reader at http://google.com/reader), share comments on interesting posts, and monitor the results achieved over time.

Join Forums and Groups

Just as blogs can reach your target audience, online groups and forums can also be a great place to connect with potential customers. When you join a group or forum, it's important that you get involved. Answer questions from other members, share useful information, and demonstrate your authority. Be sure to avoid blatantly selling. Instead, find subtle ways to mention what you do, like sharing an example about how you helped a client. If you're there providing value, members will notice. They will also notice if you're clearly there to do nothing but sell, sell, sell.

You can find all kinds of groups on LinkedIn and Facebook, as well as via http://groups.google.com and http://groups.yahoo.com. Search these sites for keywords related to your industry to find active groups that cover your area of interest. You can also search Google for industry keywords plus "group" or "forum" to uncover even more resources.

Write Articles

Article marketing has long been one of my favorite online marketing strategies. You can promote your business by writing articles for other people's websites and e-newsletters. In exchange, the site owner should include your brief author bio (50 words or fewer) along with your website link. You can also submit your articles to print publications. You'll learn more about this strategy in the Content Marketing chapter.

Author a Book

One of the most powerful business cards you will ever have is a book. It instantly establishes you as an authority in your field, reaching potential clients far and wide. A book can open the doors to speaking engagements, media interviews, consulting clients, and even corporate sponsorships. If you're a financial advisor and you meet with a client for the first time, imagine the power of handing over a copy of your book. Few of your competitors will be able to compete with that.

You can also hand out books at trade shows, give away an ebook version to people who sign up for your mailing list, or mail a copy to a hard-to-reach contact. Consider giving books to alliance partners and empower them to give copies away to prospects they refer to you.

Writing a book doesn't have to be as hard as it sounds. I have provided you with simple steps to get it done in the chapter on Building Your Audience Offline.

Start Speaking

Commanding the attention of an audience while you educate and entertain them is a powerful way to attract new business. The key is to develop speaking topics that appeal to your target audience. For example, if you're a life coach whose niche is working with busy moms, you could develop a presentation on work/life balance (rumor has it that balance is possible!) and offer tips for women to find more joy at work and at home.

Whatever your topic, there will be no shortage of opportunities to speak. You can reach out to service clubs like Rotary or Kiwanis, local chambers of commerce, trade associations, schools, retirement communities, and groups on Meetup.com. Most groups that meet on a regular basis feature speakers and are always in need of fresh, new topics. You can also expand your speaking to other businesses, or even conduct your own workshops and classes either locally or online.

Deliver White Papers and Reports

Special reports and white papers make excellent marketing collateral. These are typically informational documents that teach the reader how to do something or provide valuable data. If you're a business attorney, imagine if instead of handing a prospect a boring sales brochure, you gave them your report called 20 Biggest Risks for Retail Businesses. You would have the chance to educate them, while also helping them understand why they need your services.

These documents can be delivered in PDF format directly from your website or via email, or they can be printed and handed out at events.

Make Your Collateral Worth Keeping

In the spirit of delivering information to your prospects and clients, consider how you can develop quick tips and print them on your marketing collateral. Instead of standard business cards, I use the folded-over version. Inside, you will find 10 tips called "The Rules of Engagement for Content Marketing." These are handy suggestions that always elicit a response when I hand over my business card.

I also love to print tips on oversized postcards. These are great for mailing to prospects, handing out at events, or as inserts when mailing a package. My objective is to give prospects something that they will keep and perhaps even post on the wall in their office. Then, when they're ready for my services, they will remember who to call! Incidentally, you can do the same thing with folded booklets, standard-sized postcards, bookmarks, coffee mugs, or magnets.

Be a Leader

As an authority in your field, you should also demonstrate your leadership in your niche community. You can do this by heading up an existing group or trade association, or—my favorite—start your own group.

In 2006 I launched The Sacramento Speakers Network through Meetup.com. At the time, my goal was simply to network with other speakers in my area and see how we could support each other. We launched with a whopping five people in a Starbucks, though today we're the largest business-related network on Meetup in the Sacramento area.

Running this group has given me a tremendous amount of visibility in my local business community and has brought me speaking invitations and plenty of clients. And remember, even if you're pursuing a global audience, there could be a goldmine of clients available to you in the community where you live. What kind of group could you lead?

It All Begins with Great Content

At the heart of everything you do online is the content you create. With the evolution of the internet and social media, good content is more important than ever because it allows you to demonstrate your authority in your field and stand out from the competition. Good content can bring you website traffic and can dazzle prospects and existing customers. Following are some benefits of content.

Increase Website Traffic

Early on I realized that the more content I added to my site, the more traffic the site received. Then I discovered why: Google loves content.

The more articles and blog posts and content you have on your site, the more reasons you give Google to find you.

Because I've been running BusinessInfoGuide.com since 2004, the site has more than 1,000 pages of content—and many of those pages dominate in the search engines. If you search Google for "how to start a gym," you'll discover our industry guide page with resources for starting your own gym or fitness center. You'll get similar results if you search "how to start a travel agency" or "how to use Google alerts." These articles bring people in to the site, and then lead them to view other content, sign up for our newsletter, subscribe to the blog, and ultimately buy books and other products.

If you are a professional organizer and you write an article on how to organize a kitchen pantry or you produce a video demonstration and post it on YouTube, the next time someone searches for that topic, there is a good chance Google is going to display your article and/or video. Of course, that all depends on how many other sites have similar content, but the fact is that it doesn't take long for Google to start giving your web pages priority placement if you're adding new content on a regular basis. New content tells Google that your site is fresh and relevant, and thus Google places a higher priority on your pages, which is why news sites receive such prominent placement in Google searches.

Next, imagine that a busy work-from-home mom searches for "how to organize my kitchen pantry" and she comes across your article or video. That leads her to your website, where she discovers the many resources that you have to offer, and follows your call to action by signing up for your newsletter (she can't wait to read your bonus report!). While there, she sees that you wrote a book so she quickly purchases that, too. Within a few weeks, she calls to schedule an appointment with you. You've just converted a prospect into a client, with a little help from the power of content and Google.

Content is powerful for search engine optimization (SEO), making it far easier to show up in search results when someone is looking for topics that you write about. You'll learn more about SEO later in this book, but for now know that simply adding content on a regular basis (a minimum of twice each week, though more is better) is one of the most effective ways to bring traffic to your site.

Build Brand Recognition

Great content gets shared online via social media and social bookmarking sites. As your content is shared by viewers, you will have more and more eyeballs viewing your content and learning about you—as the authority in your field.

You can also become a regular contributor or columnist for any number of websites, where you can have even greater reach. I am a blogger for Forbes, which has been a great opportunity to get known with their readership. I also distribute articles through various content directories, trade publications, industry-specific websites, and print publications. Without a doubt this kind of exposure helps me build recognition and attract new people into my business.

You can build brand recognition for your business by sharing funny videos, writing and distributing great articles, writing guest blog posts for partner sites, producing compelling videos, posting podcasts for download, and any other way you can distribute content online. The goal is to ultimately get repeat exposure with your target audience. When you are seen and heard repeatedly in places where your audience spends time, they will begin to notice.

Impress Prospects

Great content can help you close deals. Imagine you are a business coach and a prospect is searching for a business coach online. She comes across an article you wrote and that leads her back to your website where she finds an entire archive of articles you've written, free downloads, and a virtual library of information. The prospect is so impressed with all of your work that she stops her search for a business coach and calls you on the spot.

This same scenario can apply to a business broker, life coach, virtual assistant, attorney, health practitioner, and just about any business that produces great content.

Attract Media Opportunities

Without a doubt, one of the biggest benefits of my blog is the media coverage it has attracted over the years. When the recession was just beginning, I wrote a lot of blog posts on how I was going to "reject the recession." I even printed up buttons and handed them out at events! Unfortunately, my passionate pleas to conduct business as usual despite the recession didn't exactly have an impact on the economy at large, but it did have an impact on generating media coverage. I was asked to conduct countless interviews and even had an appearance on Sunrise 7, Australia's version of the *Today* show. Reporters look for sources via online searches and when you demonstrate your authority in your field, you will inevitably attract these kinds of opportunities.

Types of Content You Can Create

Content can be distributed in more ways than ever—through your website or blog, other websites and blogs, social media sites, social bookmarking sites, content directories, and more. And it doesn't stop there. Your content can also be distributed in print publications or in tangible product form, such as a book, CD, or DVD.

Here are examples of the types of content you can create:

❖ Blog posts on your own blog

❖ Blog posts for other blogs

❖ Articles for your site

❖ Articles distributed to other websites

❖ Articles distributed to print publications (newspapers, magazines, newsletters)

❖ Video demonstration

❖ Funny or controversial video

❖ Before and after photos of work you've done

❖ Before and after videos

❖ Humorous or inspiring photos

❖ Client success stories/case studies

- ❖ Ebook
- ❖ Book (e.g., trade paperback)
- ❖ Booklets (folded over and stapled)
- ❖ Workbooks
- ❖ Fliers/One-sheets
- ❖ Special report
- ❖ White paper
- ❖ Databases with compiled information
- ❖ Upcoming event announcement
- ❖ Reports from an event you attended
- ❖ Book reviews/recommendations
- ❖ Recommended products
- ❖ Recommended services
- ❖ Tips for doing something better
- ❖ How-to suggestions
- ❖ Inspirational advice
- ❖ Breaking news alerts
- ❖ Leads for opportunities (media, clients, jobs, etc.)
- ❖ Requests for participation (guest posts on your blog, speaker for an event you're hosting, etc.)
- ❖ Photos from a recent event
- ❖ Teleseminars
- ❖ Webinars
- ❖ Contest announcements
- ❖ Special sales, offers, and discounts (delivered sparingly)
- ❖ Request for audience feedback
- ❖ A compelling question you want answered
- ❖ Anything offered for free

- ❖ Insider tips that people won't find anywhere else
- ❖ Your opinion on just about anything with target audience appeal
- ❖ Other people's content (by your customers, peers, or open call for content)

Outlets for Distributing Content

- ❖ Your website
- ❖ Your blog
- ❖ Social media networks
- ❖ Social media groups/forums
- ❖ Other websites (industry-specific, trade association, media, etc.)
- ❖ Other blogs (guest blog posts)
- ❖ Other social media outlets (when others share your content with their networks)
- ❖ Online forums (such as LinkedIn Groups)
- ❖ Article directories (ezinearticles.com, ideamarketers.com)
- ❖ Press release distribution sites (prweb.com)
- ❖ Print publications (magazines, newspapers, newsletters)
- ❖ Email marketing (your own mailing list)
- ❖ Other email marketing outlets (partners share your content in their newsletters)
- ❖ Video content sites (youtube.com, vimeo.com)
- ❖ Social bookmarking sites (digg.com)

Entrepreneur Interview
Name: Karl W. Palachuk

Business name: Small Biz Thoughts
Website URL: http://www.smallbizthoughts.com
Social media links:

> http://www.facebook.com/karlpalachuk
> http://www.twitter.com/karlpalachuk
> http://www.linkedin.com/in/karlpalachuk

Tell us about your business and what you do:

My business is based on my experience as a technology consultant. I write books, blogs, and newsletters for computer consultants. I also put on seminars and trainings, many of which are sponsored by vendors trying to get visibility within my target market.

As a result of the variety of income streams we have, we are able to sell website advertising, blog posts, and training time. I am also a paid speaker, appearing at 15-20 paid events per year.

Who is your target audience?

My audience consists primarily of small-business technology consultants who want to be better at running their businesses. This audience refers to itself as SMB (small and medium business) consultants. As a successful SMB consultant, I am seen as an "insider" rather than a stranger who wants to sell into this group.

Eventually, I developed a second audience: large companies that want to sell their products and service to (and through) the SMB consultants that made up my existing audience. Three years ago, about 5% of my revenue came from selling advertising to these companies. Now it constitutes 55% of my revenue.

How did you get started in your business?

As with so many entrepreneurs, I started my consulting business when I became disillusioned with working for corporate America. I started with one major contract and gradually transitioned to having several smaller contracts. Eventually, I hired a staff to help me deliver services.

Based on my experience as a consultant, I wrote a book about some specific processes we used to standardize service delivery. Rather than selling it like a "book," I sold it as a tool to make more money. As a tool, I was able to sell the book for a very high price.

In order to sell the book, I started traveling and speaking to consultants all over the world. After that, I helped develop a new way of delivering technical consulting and made the circuit promoting this view of business. That led to more books, more travel, more speaking, etc. Eventually, I built a large following within the well-connected technical niche.

What are some of the best tactics you have used to build your audience and establish your authority online?

I would say there are three primary tactics that helped me establish myself as an expert in my field.

One of the most successful tactics I used was cooperation: I made friends with a handful of people that I thought were "rising stars" in the community that evolved online. In various combinations of 2-4 people at a time, we appeared on stage together at events. We promoted each other. We sold each other's products when appropriate.

We were, to be honest, like the Rat Pack for computer consulting. As individuals, and as a group, the combination of activities that we engaged in amplified the expert status of everyone in the group. At one event, six of us put on a show, released six new books at once, and sold more than $30,000 worth of product in two hours.

A second successful tactic was podcasting. I appeared on a friend's podcast in 2007. His ratings for the podcast tripled that day and I decided that I had a voice in the community. So I started my own podcast, which became very popular. In fact, many people have told me that they make all their new employees listen to my old podcasts.

After two years, I re-branded and re-packaged the podcast. At that point I started charging a monthly fee for members to download the podcast. After a year, I doubled the cost. In January 2012, we changed the format again in order to keep it fresh. It continues to be a money-making venture and has new subscribers every month.

A third successful tactic has been blogging. I started blogging in 2006. At that time, I decided that my blog had to provide information that was not being provided elsewhere. Many blogs and websites offer free technical training and information. Nerds love to show how nerdy they are, so they freely share technical information. My niche had to do with the business side of running a business. I blog about profit and loss statements, hiring practices, service contracts, and other *business* topics.

One of my favorite blogging strategies is to start a "series" of blog posts that build on one another and refer back to previous posts in the series. It might be a series of three or four, or a much longer series. One series called *Managed Services in a Month* eventually became the basis for a book. Another series appears every Friday and has become a consistent draw for new blog readers.

How has social media impacted your business? Any success stories you can share?

I primarily use social media as a means of broadcasting content. I'm a firm believer that 95% of the people on social media are primarily consumers of information and 5% are primarily producers of information. I am a producer.

I send out regular posts to Twitter, Facebook, and LinkedIn. The only forum I actually check in on and post to in real life is Facebook. I post pictures and observations in real time, and I make comments on things I find there.

In the big picture, I believe the social media networks are great for building credibility and getting people onto my mailing list. As an actual sales tool (asking for money), I don't find them very effective. But I can lure people onto my mailing lists, and then sell from there.

Do you engage in any communities and if so, how has that impacted your business?

I have always participated in online communities. Yahoo Groups are still surprisingly big in the technical communities. I have had good luck participating in the groups. As a frequent contributor, I am once again an "insider" when it comes time to ask people to buy what I'm selling. If I only dropped in to ask for a sale every three months, I would remain an outsider.

What advice would you offer to readers who want to promote their business online?

The most important advice I have is to understand that your online platform is a *marketing* platform. You need to integrate it into your sales process. You need to use it to promote your sales goals. But please do not think that blogging and social media will do your selling for you. These tools will soften up the prospects, but they will not sell for you.

You will always have to make your own sales by engaging people, making proposals, and asking for money. I recommend that you consider your company's strategy for moving from the online marketing funnel into the email- and telephone-based sales funnel.

If you were starting your business over today, is there anything you would do differently?

Oh my goodness …

Quick Tip

I was thrilled when I watched the launch of an online forum inviting people who "avoid excessive hype and snake-oil offers" to collaborate and share information. Launched and managed by Darren Rowse, Brian Clark, Sonia Simone, and Chris Brogan, http://thirdtribemarketing.com is a community for hype-free internet marketers—and one of the smartest movements I've seen online.

Chapter Three
Build Your Audience and Engage Community

"We must remember that one determined person can make a significant difference, and that a small group of determined people can change the course of history."
—Sonia Johnson

A s human beings, we need community. Community allows us to connect with people. Think about your involvement in your church, your alumni association, trade association, your kid's sports league, or the neighborhood where you live. Community gives us a sense of belonging. According to Dan Buettner, author of *Thrive*, joining a group where you show up each month gives you a happiness boost at the equivalent of doubling your income. Yes, we crave connection.

In business, communities provide a way to connect with your audience. Once you've defined your niche audience, you can do one of two things: engage in existing communities that reach them or start a community that attracts them.

General Networking vs. Community Networking

In the world of entrepreneurship, there's no shortage of networking opportunities. Every community has networking groups, whether through the chamber of commerce, trade association, or an organized networking group such as BNI or Le Tip. Business networking can be a great way to get known in your community, which can lead to referrals, alliances, and other opportunities. However, these general networking groups can have a limited reach.

For Karl Palachuk, an author and speaker who markets to IT consultants, spending time in a weekly business group wouldn't net nearly the same return as his time spent with technology user groups (both online and in-person) where the audience consists solely of IT consultants. As a result, you won't find him attending general leads groups.

General business groups can be a good place to reach a wide variety of fellow entrepreneurs, but this strategy lacks focus on a target audience. Generally speaking, networking groups are good for people who want to market to other entrepreneurs. Businesses that traditionally do well in these groups include bankers, business and life coaches, real estate professionals, financial advisors, web designers, and insurance agents.

What would happen if you took your networking a step further and also spent time in the communities where you want to do business?

For example, if you own a marketing firm that focuses on the dental market, it would make perfect sense to network in dental communities. You could seek out trade associations, online groups, and dental forums. If you're a graphic designer with a niche in working with product catalogs, then your networking efforts should be focused on retail associations and related online forums.

Also look to communities for referral partners. For example, if you own a video production firm and good referral partners for you are marketing and PR professionals, then get involved in their communities. Join their trade associations and make an impact.

These communities are also great places to demonstrate your authority by speaking, joining the leadership team, or writing articles for their newsletters. Once you focus your community marketing efforts, the rewards can be substantial.

Community Marketing Methods

When aiming your marketing efforts at communities, the first consideration is your niche audience. You want to figure out where they spend their time, what their interests are, and where you can find them. Following are some places to begin your search.

Online Communities

Since the advent of the internet, online communities have made it easy to connect with other like-minded individuals. Online forums foster conversations on specific topics related to the community at hand. You can find forums on just about everything, from parenting and technology to diet and butterflies.

If there's an interest, there's a forum. A quick Google search on your topic of interest plus the word "forum" should lead to all kinds of possibilities.

Social Media Groups

Facebook and LinkedIn host thousands of online groups where once again you will find a diverse array of topics. One of my favorite examples is something I stumbled across on Facebook: The Honda Civic Owners Club. Yep, that's right. If you own a Honda Civic, a large network awaits you. Most interesting is that this group is moderated by a Honda auto parts distributor. Talk about brilliant marketing. Attract your ideal audience by building a welcoming community, and then serve their needs.

For more business-focused groups, look to LinkedIn. Here you will find groups for human resources professionals (led by an HR trade association), chief information officers (led by *CIO* magazine), and nonfiction authors (led by yours truly). There are also alumni groups, groups based in specific locations, and all kinds of specialty niches.

Joining a group is just the first step. If you really want to build business connections, you must engage in the group. Participate in the community forum by answering questions asked by members. Also ask questions, share news and articles, and get involved. Each group on LinkedIn features a sidebar with "Top Influencers This Week," showing the photo and name for each person who contributed the most content. Showing up here gives you visibility with active members and demonstrates your authority in the subject matter.

I recently responded to a question in the nonfiction authors network that I lead on LinkedIn. I simply gave some advice, which I do frequently. Another member followed my post with this:

Stephanie didn't mention this herself, but you should know that her book Booked Up: How to Write, Publish, and Promote a Book to Grow Your Business *is wonderful and has a lot of additional promotion ideas.*

You can't pay for that kind of marketing, and when you get involved in a community where the members are familiar with you and your work, this kind of thing happens all the time.

Also, if there's more than one group focused on your topic, find out where you can make the most impact. It may be harder to make an impact on a group with 10,000+ members. A smaller group may actually have more advantages since it will be easier to stand out.

Facebook Fan Pages

Many businesses view Facebook pages simply as online business cards, but they can be so much more. Smart companies use their pages to engage and build community. One company that does this really well is Victoria's Secret. Look up their page and you will find that they have millions of fans. Their Facebook wall is full of comments because they ask their audience to participate, share their feedback, and write about their shopping experiences. Victoria's Secret has a captive audience of customers and they keep them engaged with questions, special promotions, and details about new product lines.

Consider how you can engage your audience on Facebook. Can you share useful content, ask for feedback, invite fans to share videos or photos, or otherwise increase the number of interactions you have there?

Professional Groups

Beyond trade associations there are other kinds of professional groups and organizations. These can include church groups, sporting leagues, political groups, knitting clubs, moms' groups, book clubs, nonprofits, and service organizations such as Rotary or Kiwanis.

The point is that there are a wide variety of groups with a broad base of members—members who could make great clients for your business. For example, if you're a therapist who works with kids, you could join moms' groups or be a speaker for them.

Geographic Communities

For some businesses, it's all about location. Real estate agents are a great example. In this profession, often the goal is to meet as many people as possible. And while this can lead to referrals, I'd suggest that a better strategy would be to focus on specific neighborhoods. Join or start groups within a specific geography to get to know the residents and people who do business there. You could even head up the launch of a Neighborhood Watch program or focus on community activism.

Build Your Own Online Community

If you can turn your website into a community destination for your target audience, you will begin spinning gold. A simple five-page brochure website is not likely to draw people in by the thousands, but an online community with resources and valuable information can in itself become a client-generating machine.

Chris Garrett is a consultant specializing in blogging and social media, yet when you visit his website (www.chrisg.com) you'll find far more than the standard five-page brochure site. Chris has made his blog a go-to resource for people interested in blogging and social media. It's loaded with interesting how-to content, the same stuff he teaches his clients. Why would he give away so much information? Because most people still want to be guided through the process, or they simply want someone else to do it for them.

Important note: Don't be afraid to give away your best ideas. This builds a loyal audience who will be MORE likely to hire you as a result!

Chris also offers a free ebook giveaway to new clients, actively responds to those who comment on his blog, and has a strong social media presence. He's also co-author with Darren Rowse of the book *ProBlogger: Secrets for Blogging Your Way to a Six-Figure Income.* You can bet that his rates for consulting and speaking have gone through the roof as he's increased his authority in his field and cultivated his community.

Consider how your website can become a community for your target audience. It can include any number of features such as articles, blogs, interviews with others in your field, client case studies, how-to guides, white papers, reports, ebooks, printable forms, fun quizzes, or a forum. You also don't have to create all of the content yourself. Invite others to contribute articles and interviews. Hold contests, engage your audience, and make it valuable and fun.

Imagine how different your business could be if you tapped into the power of community and your customers came looking for you!

Strategic Referrals

Referrals are at the heart of many businesses for good reason. When someone refers a client to you, half the work is already done. When you've been recommended by a trusted source, the sale will be far easier to close than a cold lead.

With traditional business networking groups, referrals are a big focus. It seems the goal is to meet as many people as you can in hopes that they know someone who needs your services. But what would happen if you focused on building more strategic referral relationships?

For my publishing business, book coaches and ghostwriters make great referral partners because they interact with my prospects right before they need my services. I am constantly reaching out to these businesses to discuss how we can work together. It helps that we don't offer coaching or ghostwriting services and can in turn refer business back to them.

To develop more strategic referral partners, I had my marketing assistant research coaches and ghostwriters online and then send them an introductory email asking if they would like to be listed as a resource on my website. This was a fantastic way to develop a win-win situation and strategic partnerships that lead to client referrals. As a bonus, that directory page I created on my site shows up at the top of Google when you search for "book coach," and that alone has brought client leads to my business.

When looking for alliance partners, think about who reaches your clients before you. If you're a divorce attorney, a good source would be marriage therapists because they often see clients just before "the big decision." An accountant who works with retailers could partner with people who sell merchant card services (credit card processing) or commercial real estate agents who lease space to new businesses. A personal trainer could partner with a nutritionist or life coach.

Brainstorm a list of potential referral partners, and then consider the best ways to get introduced to each other and work together. Here are some considerations:

- ❖ Can you send introductions via email or LinkedIn?

- ❖ Can you mail them a copy of your book?

- ❖ Do you have a report or postcard with tips that you can leave in their lobby?

- ❖ Do they belong to a trade association that you can join?

- ❖ Would they be interested in receiving a referral fee?

- ❖ Can you create a win-win situation by also referring business to them?

- ❖ Can you add a directory on your website where they can be listed?

When I moved into my house, my real estate agent left a booklet she had compiled of local businesses. I thought that was brilliant. I was new to the town and found it really helpful. No doubt it also made her a valuable contact in the eyes of those she recommended, and in turn I'm certain that those businesses sent her referrals as well. Think outside of the box! Could you create a directory of resources and partner with a series of businesses to co-promote each other?

Once you discover strategic referrals and turn up the client generation furnace, you'll never look at referrals the same way again!

Entrepreneur Interview
Name: Melinda F. Emerson "SmallBizLady"

Business name: Quintessence Multimedia
Website URL: www.succeedasyourownboss.com
Social media links:

> www.twitter.com/smallbizlady
> www.twitter.com/smallbizchat
> http://linkedin.com/melindaemerson
> http://facebook.com/smallbizlady

Tell us about your business and what you do:

I am a national small-business expert and professional writer. My nickname is SmallBizLady and my mission is to end small-business failure. I am the best-selling author of *Become Your Own Boss in 12 Months*. I teach would-be and existing entrepreneurs how to start, grow, or reinvent a successful small business. My company develops audio, video, and written content to help entrepreneurs learn the business of running a small business. I am also a professional speaker and corporate trainer on small-business startup, business development, and social media marketing. I have the fastest-growing small-business brand on the internet and *Forbes Magazine* named me the #1 woman for entrepreneurs to follow on Twitter. I host #SmallBizChat Wednesdays on Twitter from 8-9 p.m. ET, which provides a live weekly forum for entrepreneurs to get answers and advice. My blog www.succeedasyourownboss.com is a resource that provides daily advice on how to start and grow a profitable and sustainable small business.

Who is your target audience?

Professional women 30+ who are married, mothers, and Christians.

How did you get started in your business?

I started out my career as a TV news producer. When I was in college, Oprah Winfrey started Harpo Studios. Her actions to become a businesswoman inspired me to consider entrepreneurship. I was a sophomore in college, and I believed that one day I could, too, start my own production company. But I knew that I needed to learn the business first. So I spent six years in the television industry as a news producer; then I started my first company, Quintessence Multimedia, in 1999. Quintessence provides social media strategy, marketing consulting, video production, web development, and multimedia content development. In 2007, I started MFE Consulting, LLC to launch my professional speaking, writing, and consulting business. We work with Fortune 500 companies and media entities that need content and advice on small-business ownership.

What are some of the best tactics you have used to build your audience and establish your authority online?

Twitter and my blog are the two best things I have used to build my brand online. I was an early user of Twitter. I started in 2008. That is also where I got my nickname SmallBizLady, which is the best branding accident that ever happened to me. Since my name was taken, I had to create a new brand that told people who I was and what I stood for. I kicked around a few ideas with a social media strategist and we decided on @SmallBizLady.

In early 2009, I launched #Smallbizchat, my weekly Twitter talk show where I answer small-business questions. Once I built a community of small-business owners on Twitter, I launched my blog: www.succeedasyoutrownboss.com. I started out blogging two days a week and it grew from there. Today, I have more than 100,000 followers and one of the largest small-business brands on Twitter.

How has social media impacted your business? Any success stories you can share?

Social media is the secret sauce in my business. I am a walking, talking social media brand. I reinvented my business entirely using social media marketing. But it took time; it did not start raining money the minute I started using Twitter, LinkedIn, Facebook, and blogging. Social media is all about attraction marketing. Rather than chasing your target clients, you can attract them to you by positioning yourself as a valuable resource through content. You must create your own signature content and share other expert content.

Every professional writing assignment I have had since 2010 has come to me from a contact on Twitter—I did not pitch a single assignment. My media and speaking appearances have come the same way. I am often asked if I have a publicist; I do not. I have my signature content and I am very good at promoting it.

I also think launching #Smallbizchat was key to my success. By hosting a weekly chat, I have engaged directly with my community every week for years. I am also the convener of the conversation, and that is an extremely influential position to have as an information marketer.

Do you engage in any communities and if so, how has that impacted your business?

I have two communities that I convene: #Smallbizchat on Twitter and Smallbizchat on LinkedIn. I also interact with more 50 groups through LinkedIn to share my content and answer questions. I also use http://focus.com, an expert answers site, to promote my expertise by answering specific questions about social media and small business startup.

What role does content play in your marketing strategy?

Content is everything to my brand. I develop articles, Q&A interviews, videos, and blogtalkradio interviews for my own blog. I also blog and create videos for http://secondact.com, http://smallbiztrends.com, and write for *Black Enterprise* and *Essence* magazine. I develop blog content for corporate website clients, too, including Pitney Bowes, Deluxe Corporation, and Verizon.

What advice would you offer to readers who want to promote their business online?

They need to know who their target customer is first. Then they need to figure out where that customer hangs out online and be a part of the conversation. Authenticity is essential to success in social media. Use your picture, not your company logo, in social media profiles. Understand the concept of "give to get." Help others first, promote other people's content, and then promote your own content. They need to seek—"like, know, and trust"—first before any selling is done. If you are going to start blogging, make sure you can keep it up. Consistency counts for a whole lot when building a brand online. Remember, it takes at least seven quality contacts before you can approach a social media contact about commerce.

If you were starting your business over today, is there anything you would do differently?

I would not do anything differently.

Is there anything else you would like to add?

There is a triple return on investment (ROI) in social media:

> **Return on investment.** The investment to measure is time, not dollars, and a smart social media program returns the time you put in with customers, prospects, and word-of-mouth referrals.

> **Return on influence.** By sharing quality content, small-business owners build influence, which they can leverage online and off.

> **Return on identity.** Everything in social media is about brand identity. You can hurt your brand as much as you can grow your brand. Proceed with a strategy.

Quick Tip

Want funding for creative projects such as your next book, film, or work of art? Check out www.kickstarter.com, a crowd-sourced funding option where supporters can pledge from $1 to thousands of dollars in exchange for perks that you offer (such as a signed copy of your book, one-on-one consulting, or access to an event you're hosting). A similar option is www.indiegogo.com.

Chapter Four

Turn Your Website into a Client Conversion Machine

"Don't let the fear of the time it will take to accomplish something stand in the way of your doing it.
The time will pass anyway; we might just as well put that passing time to the best possible use."
—Earl Nightingale

The content on your website is as important, if not more important, than the actual site design. You could have the most beautiful website design, but if the content—your website copy—doesn't deliver the right message, then your website will fail to do its job.

I recommend hiring a professional web copywriter to help you develop the best sales message possible. You can take a chance on writing it yourself or hiring a writer whose primary focus is writing articles or other types of content, but writing great web copy is truly an art within itself. Ideally, you want to use the services of someone who has experience.

However, if you want to do it yourself, following are some guidelines to make it easier and more effective.

How to Write Great Website Copy

Easy to Read — Internet users have short attention spans. Nobody wants to sit and read endless paragraphs of text, and studies show that users scan web pages to find relevant information. Your pages should include plenty of headings, sub-headings, and bulleted lists to be read easily on a computer screen.

Know Your Audience — Who is your target demographic? Are you targeting high-end clients? Busy working moms? Or maybe you want to reach cost-conscious clients? Your content should address the needs and desires of your target audience.

Be Concise — The key to effective sales copy is to get the message across in as few words as possible. When it comes to a website, it all goes back to the attention span of the reader. Messages should be clear and tightly written. If you want to expand on a topic, offer a brief summary with an option to "click here to learn more about XYZ topic" that opens in a new page.

Use Simple Language — Newspaper reporters are required to write at a tenth-grade level and for good reason. Unfortunately, this is how the majority of readers can relate. It is important to avoid using industry jargon, acronyms, or slang that not every site visitor will understand. Sadly, the general public cannot easily comprehend "big words," so you should stick with the basics.

Stick to Present Tense, 2nd Person — Readers should identify with what they are reading. When you speak to them directly instead of in general terms, the copy has more impact. Use the power of "you" phrases whenever possible.

Instead of:
***Our clients** appreciate our attention to the details.*

Use the following:
***You will** appreciate our attention to the details.*

Describe Benefits Instead of Features — One of the biggest marketing mistakes you can make is listing the features of a product or service instead of the *benefits*. Buyers want to know what's in it for them. They want to know how this product or service will solve a problem, make life easier, save time, or save money.

Feature: Hundreds of designs to choose from.
Benefit: You can choose the design that best fits your unique needs.

Feature: Life coaching for busy moms.
Benefit: You will learn to regain control of your schedule and add more joy to your busy life.

Overcome Objections or Barriers to Entry — When visitors view your website, you have a unique opportunity to overcome possible objections quickly. For example, if some visitors assume that they can't afford your services, you can indicate in your web copy that you offer special promotions and discounts for students and those who sign up to receive your newsletter. Consider any potential barriers that buyers may have and address them early on.

Include a Call to Action — A standard brochure-type website that simply tells visitors what you do is not enough. Your site should ask visitors to take action. Do you want them to make a purchase immediately? Sign up for your mailing list? Fill out an online form? Call for a quote? Once you understand the goal, a simple change that will make a big difference is to add a call to action to each and every page on your site. Here are some examples:

Get your free sample now by filling out our online form.

Call us now for a no-obligation consultation.

Sign up for our newsletter and receive a bonus report: 20 Ways to Bring Romance Back to Your Marriage.

Do you notice what these statements have in common? They provide specific instructions for what the reader should do next. It's amazing how this simple addition to the content on your web pages can make such a difference. Simply asking can ensure that visitors take action before they move on to something else and forget to return later.

Repeat Important Details — The majority of site visitors won't read every word on every page of your website. Don't be afraid to duplicate content and descriptions on pages. Not only can this be useful for search engine optimization (as you will learn in the next section), but it will ensure that site visitors are aware of featured services, products, or any other details that are important to convey.

E-Commerce Implementation

Making your products or services available for sale online can quickly generate new revenue for many types of businesses. Even selling just a few items can have an impact on your bottom line.

A couple of years ago, my father's birthday was approaching and I decided to get him a gift certificate to his favorite golf course. I found the website and searched through their pages, but didn't see anywhere to buy a gift certificate. Begrudgingly, I picked up the phone and called the pro shop and to my amazement, they informed me that not only could I not buy a gift certificate online, but they wouldn't accept my order over the phone—I had to come in to their office to make a purchase!

I live hours away from my father and there was no way I was making a trip to that golf course or any other business to purchase a gift card. The moral of this story: A gift certificate is an easy item to make available for sale online. You can also add information products, such as special reports or downloadable workbooks. If your prices for services are straightforward, it may also make sense to add shopping cart buttons and sell them directly from your site as well.

Everything about your site should make it easy for prospects to do business with you. If you host special events or workshops, make sure you add a way for people to register directly on your site; otherwise, you will definitely miss out on buyers.

Shopping Carts and Credit Card Processing

If you decide to sell products and/or services from your website, you're going to need a way to automate the sales and payment process. There are dozens of shopping cart programs available, depending on your needs.

PayPal

PayPal (http://paypal.com) offers a user-friendly shopping cart solution that you can implement on your existing website, allowing you to process credit card payments for purchases. It doesn't cost anything to set up and there are no monthly fees for basic services, though like all credit card processors, PayPal keeps a small percentage of each transaction. PayPal's shopping cart solution is quick and easy to implement and should be sufficient if you are selling just a few products or services through your site (like gift certificates).

PayPal will allow you to create custom shopping cart buttons with HTML code that you can insert into your website. Once a payment is processed with a site visitor, the visitor will receive a confirmation email and you will receive an email notification about the sale.

Funds collected are deposited to your PayPal account. You can receive a debit card with instant access to your account. You can also transfer funds from your PayPal account directly into your bank account—the transfer takes several business days. Also, buyers do not need to have a PayPal account to make a purchase. For its ease of use and convenience, PayPal can be a great solution for basic shopping cart services.

As a side note, PayPal also offers two other useful services. The Virtual Terminal service allows you to manually process credit cards from your desktop by keying in credit card information. There is also an invoicing tool so you can send digital invoices to customers that they can pay online.

Google Checkout

Similar to PayPal, Google offers an e-commerce solution that is growing in popularity. Google Checkout (http://checkout.google.com/sell) allows you to add shopping cart buttons to your website, and shoppers have an option to pay via credit card.

Also similar to PayPal, Google charges a transaction fee based on your total sales volume and provides HTML code to add to your site. Google Checkout also integrates with Google Adwords (pay-per-click ads), and advertisers receive merchant processing rewards each month.

1ShoppingCart

For a robust solution, check out 1ShoppingCart.com (www.1shoppingcart.com). This company offers shopping cart solutions, merchant card processing, secure digital product delivery, auto responders for email management, the ability to set up your own affiliate program (offer others commission for selling your products), and the ability to create special discount codes. If you're selling digital products, this service is a good option because it's designed to manage digital product delivery.

e-junkie

If you need a robust shopping cart solution that is also cost-effective, visit http://e-junkie.com. This service offers most of the features of competitors and has an active affiliate directory so if you want to allow others to sell your digital products and earn a commission, you can take advantage of their network.

Additional Resources:

> Amazon Payments: https://payments.amazon.com
> Practice Pay Solutions: http://practicepaysolutions.com/
> Infusionsoft: http://infusionsoft.com

Converting Site Visitors into Buyers

Once you have your website up and running and a shopping cart system in place, the next step is to make sure your website does its job. Here are some tips to get your sales cranking:

- ❖ Make it easy for visitors to find your products and services. Easy site navigation is important, so make sure your primary product page is listed on the main navigation menu for your site.

- ❖ Cross-promote products throughout your site. For example, on your services web page, you might add an anchored link that says, "Purchase a Gift Certificate for Consulting Services."

- ❖ List all of your products on a single shopping cart page along with separate anchored links to complete product descriptions on individual pages.

- ❖ Include real user testimonials (not the manufactured kind from friends and peers) throughout your site and on sales pages for maximum impact. Never underestimate the power of testimonials!

- ❖ Depending on your target audience, you may want to include a printable order form for people who don't want to place orders online. Give them a way to mail and fax the order to you.

❖ Make sure your purchase process is simple and easy to use. Test it out by making a purchase yourself. Are there any steps missing? Is the information confusing?

❖ Set up a thank you page. When a customer completes an order with you, make sure they are returned to a thank you page. Industry reports indicate that the thank you page is a highly effective place to up-sell additional products. For example, the thank you page could say: "People who bought product ABC also rave about product XYZ. Click here to order XYZ at 25% off!"

❖ If you are promoting multiple services or products, put a "Featured Service" section on your home page or in the sidebar of all of your web pages. Change the offer each week or month to keep it fresh and interesting.

Entrepreneur Interview
Name: Kathleen Reale

Business name: BeFreeForMe.com

Website URL: http://www.befreeforme.com

Social media links:

> http://www.facebook.com/befreeforme
> http://twitter.com/kreale
> http://www.linkedin.com/in/kathleenreale

Tell us about your business and what you do:

Befreeforme.com is the first and only website to offer coupons, savings, and samples to gluten- and food-allergy-free consumers. Befreeforme.com enables people who suffer with gluten intolerance and other food allergies to find support, recipes, reviews, articles, and coupons to effectively manage their allergies and save money in the process. We currently have more than 40,000 members. It is free to join.

Befreeforme.com is basically the marketing liaison between our clients—who are food manufacturers, distributors, retailers, and restaurants—to reach this rapidly growing demographic and their pursuit for products and savings.

Who is your target audience?

Befreeforme.com's target audience is anyone living with celiac disease (every 1 in 133 people) or food allergies (almost 4% of the U.S. population). Although not originally expected, a secondary audience—not targeted—has also expanded to include medical doctors, RN's, dieticians, grocery retailers, food marketers, and health/wellness/food bloggers—all seeking to gather more information regarding this niche market.

How did you get started in your business?

For 20 years, I ran a highly profitable and successful event marketing and in-store demonstration company (think the ladies in the supermarkets handing out food samples at your local grocer!). The company received numerous awards and was recognized by Ernst & Young as a Top Growth Business in Massachusetts. In addition, I received numerous entrepreneurial awards, including a selection as a U.S. Small Business Administration Mentor for the Women's Network for Entrepreneurial Training Program.

After living with family members with various food allergies, I received a life-altering celiac diagnosis in 2004, the same year I decided to sell the event marketing business. At this time, I began thinking of a way to merge my passion for celiac and food allergy awareness with my marketing, promotions, and business acumen.

After I was diagnosed with celiac disease, I learned what many celiac sufferers discover: living a gluten-free lifestyle takes preparation, time, and money. As I saw my family's grocery bills skyrocket, I decided to take a chance and put a twist on my "traditional" way of marketing products, and created a web-based business, befreeforme.com, a savings community for food-intolerant and food-allergy-free consumers.

What are some of the best tactics you have used to build your audience and establish your authority online?

Befreeforme.com offers offhand personal experiences of living a gluten-free lifestyle, as well as experts' opinions on various allergy-related topics. I realized right out of the gate, though, that I was not a registered dietician, medical doctor, or a trained chef, and I would need to partner with these folks to assist with blog posts and answer questions from the befreeforme.com members that I could not answer.

I have built my audience and established a rapport with them by recognizing and using my "voice" and my style. It's casual, laid-back, and fun.

I established my authority online by being "me"—a gal with celiac disease looking to save money on gluten-free foods. Other than that, I count on credible sources to take care of the medical, nutritional, and culinary questions I get from the befreeforme.com members that I cannot answer, and put a fun twist on the questions and the presentation in answering them in the process.

How has social media impacted your business? Any success stories you can share?

Shortly after starting my business, I was contacted by a national gluten-free food manufacturer to be a "guest" on a Twitter party they were sponsoring. I was thrilled that I was one of four hosts—including Elisabeth Hasselbeck, who is also a fellow celiac and author of a book regarding celiac disease.

But why did they ask me? I found out later that they asked me to be a host for their Twitter party because I marketed myself as an expert on the celiac disease lifestyle on my website, in my description of who I was on LinkedIn/Facebook/Twitter, on sales collateral/media kits, and during tradeshows/face-to-face introductions. But not only was I an expert; I was "fun, engaging, and approachable." Someone that you'd want to invite to an "in-person party," let alone a "virtual party"—someone that could connect with the celiac community and keep the conversation going.

It was great to be on the same "special guest" list as Elisabeth Hasselbeck—it was a once-in-a-lifetime opportunity that I stumbled upon because I marketed myself as the expert that I am on a gluten-free lifestyle. Words of advice? Don't be afraid to toot your own horn!

Do you engage in any communities and if so, how has that impacted your business?

In particular, I engage with a number of national celiac organizations. One in particular is the National Foundation for Celiac Awareness. They are a go-to resource for those with celiac disease. I asked to be on their list of resources on their website and they agreed. This has been a great way to get visits to the befreeforme.com website and new members referred by a credible source. Words of advice? Don't be afraid to ask!

What role does content play in your marketing strategy?

Content is a huge part of my marketing strategy. I need to keep the content on my website/blog fresh, new, and current to keep the members coming back for more.

I also realized that I need to "remind" people to visit the website. I do this by creating different email lists that members can sign up for when they join. They can opt in to receive the *every so often* coupons/deals that befreeforme.com offers from our paid advertisers, the Q&A email answered by an expert (medical professional, chef, etc.) that goes out *once or twice a month*, or the Daily Thought email that goes out *daily* and offers an inspirational quote early each morning. By doing this, I am asking for permission to reach the members more often than just once a month with a newsletter, which I think is one of the biggest mistakes people make when marketing their website. Why not ask to send out a weekly tip email, or a deal-of-the-day email?

Most important, I make sure that the email I send out has several links back to the befreeforme.com website. I do this by linking to recipes, articles, and blog posts.

Email marketing has allowed me to get more daily hits back to my website and also create revenue by selling advertising space on the emails.

What advice would you offer to readers who want to promote their business online?

There are two main things that I would advise readers to do to promote their businesses online:

1. **Be Yourself!** Whenever writing blog posts, use your own "voice." Write as if you are talking to a friend. Also, make sure the copy on your website (homepage, about us, sign-up pages, etc.) reflects who you are and the "image" you want to portray. Do you want to be the Julia Child, the Rachael Ray, or the Emeril Lagasse or your niche market? Establish who you are and stick with it!

2. **Set up ongoing blog series and stick with the schedule!**
   One of the things people ask me the most is how I come
   up with blog ideas to write about. One of the easiest ways
   is to set up a blog series and stick with it. I have an "Ask
   Shelley Case, R.D." column that is posted on my blog, and
   a link to the post is sent to members in an email the second
   Tuesday of each month. I also have a WIN-It-Wednesday
   blog contest every other Wednesday, and every week a
   Friday Favorite, which is a review of some of my favorite
   products. This keeps me on track and keeps the content on
   the blog fresh and updated.

**If you were starting your business over today, is there
anything you would do differently?**

I wish I had just jumped in and started at least a blog during the
planning stages of the befreeforme website. The one thing about
marketing on the web is that things can be changed with a click
of the mouse. I was thinking old-school marketing, which is to
make sure everything is perfect before it goes to print. With web
marketing, anything can be changed instantaneously.

Is there anything else you would like to add?

Make sure that you don't just count on Facebook or Twitter to
gain followers. Get people to your website and ask them for their
information (name, email, mailing address, and any other pertinent
information). This way, you can reach out to them directly through
email marketing—which many website marketers underutilize.

By having a large database of members (more than 40,000
members) befreeforme.com has been able to create a revenue base
with paid advertisers thorough email marketing campaigns. Also,
by knowing our members' mailing addresses, we can offer geo-
targeted email blasts and market to not just national companies,
but also geographical ones as well.

The last thing I would like to add is to have fun!

Chapter Five
Increase Website Traffic

"If you don't get noticed, you don't have anything. You just have to be noticed, but the art is in getting noticed naturally, without screaming or without tricks."
—Leo Burnett, renowned advertising executive

No matter the size of your business, a good website—one that is optimized for the search engines—can bring in new clients and keep your existing clients engaged in your business. For example, let's say you own a hair salon in Orlando. When a user searches the Internet for "hair salon in Orlando," your site should appear in the top ten results (on the first page of the search results). If that's not happening, your website strategy isn't working for you.

I see this all the time. I use the internet to locate businesses both where I live and globally. It never ceases to amaze me that if I search for something like "Dry Cleaner in Reno," only one or two websites appear, even though there are dozens of dry cleaning businesses in the area. This is a major missed opportunity!

Try This:

Go to www.google.com and search for keywords related to your business and the city where you are located. Does your business appear in the search results? Try various combinations of key terms that your target audience would use to find you. If your business isn't listed in the top ten, then you need to keep reading!

Why Search Matters

The goal for every website owner should be to appear in the top ten results on Google when someone searches for your services or products. As you may have noticed, when you search for just about anything on Google, you will usually receive tens of thousands of results. Most people scan the top ten results on the first page, find what they need, or move on. If your site shows up on page 2 or 12 or 112, it's going to be very difficult to get traffic to your site.

Before I launch into a discussion on search engine optimization (SEO), I want to mention some important points. First of all, I believe that blogging on a regular basis is *the best SEO you can get*. The more content you add to your site, the more relevant it becomes with Google and the more reasons you give Google to find you. I've said it before and I'll say it again: If you implement just one strategy from this book, it should be a blog.

Second, SEO is a hotly contested topic. You could speak to ten different SEO consultants and get ten different recommended strategies. I've decided to stick with the tried-and-true basics here—strategies that I have personally used so I know they work, and strategies that you can easily implement yourself.

SEO Basics

Search Engine Optimization (SEO) is what you do to improve your website's organic ranking with the search engines (Google, Yahoo, etc.). Since around 70% of all internet searches are conducted with Google, it's a good idea to focus on how Google ranks your site.

Google uses complex algorithms to determine a website's relevance and its ranking when a search is conducted. This section covers basic SEO strategies that have proven to be effective for Google and the other major search engines. By implementing the strategies in this chapter, you should see a noticeable impact on the placement of your website pages in the search engines.

Why Text Matters

Google uses technology called spiders to "crawl" across web pages looking for patterns in the text. This is one of the ways it determines what a website offers and how it should be categorized. This is the most basic and perhaps the most important element in gaining better placement in the search engines. So when someone searches for "massage therapist in Seattle," it is imperative that your site include this key phrase.

Every web page has a place to indicate the keywords, page title, and description. This information gets encoded in the page and is the first data that Google sees. When this data is absent or unfocused, it can hurt your site's relevance with Google.

This is also one of the biggest errors I see on most websites. Without a keyword strategy to let the search engines know what services you offer and where your business is located, you can't expect to achieve top placement in search results. There is simply too much competition out there vying for the top ten.

Using Keywords

Keywords are the heart of your SEO strategy and should include individual words and phrases that your target clients would most likely use to locate your business. For example, if you're a professional speaker and business consultant your keywords might look like this:

Professional speaker San Francisco
Professional speaker California
Professional speaker leadership
Leadership consulting
Business consulting leadership
Business consultant leadership
Leadership consultant San Francisco
Leadership consulting California

If you are targeting a local audience, including the city name in your keyword strategy is vitally important. If you serve surrounding cities, it's a good idea to include those as well. Even if you want to reach a global audience, including a key phrase for your location can be beneficial if clients may look for that information. For example, I recently landed a paid speaking engagement because the client was looking for a speaker in California and found my site. If I had omitted that information, I would have missed that opportunity.

For ideas on which keywords to use for your business, try Google's free keyword tool: https://adwords.**google**.com/select/**KeywordTool**External. *When you type in a keyword or phrase here, Google shows you related phrases and their popularity in searches. This can be valuable information for helping you understand what your customers are looking for. Also, key phrases that are wildly popular are going to be harder to compete with. You may want to focus on incorporating key phrases with slightly less popularity and more of a niche focus.*

For example, the key phrase "life coach" receives over 368,000 searches per month while "career life coach" receives 6,600. If you're a coach specializing in careers, there's still plenty of search traffic for your specialty, and it will likely be easier to show up in the search engines if you focus on that less popular search phrase.

Keywords work best when they match the *content* on your web page. So when writing your web copy, it's best to <u>repeat the most important keyword phrase throughout the page</u> two or three times. If you want your page to come up when someone searches for "Dallas massage therapist," then there should be several mentions of Dallas massage therapist throughout the text on the page. Also, when possible, use the keyword phrase in the heading and/or first paragraph of text. Google may not crawl all the way down each page, so the first two paragraphs are prime real estate.

Of course, there is a caveat to all of this. The search engines will penalize you if you try to beat the system. So don't bother repeating keywords dozens of times—they will view this as keyword stuffing and it could actually hurt your ranking or get your site removed from the search engine altogether. Google does care about keyword density. Good keyword density should add up to 4% to 7% of the content on the page, with 93% of the page for other content.

Ultimately, what you want to do is develop a keyword map for your entire site. *Each page should have its own unique set of keywords,* which allows you to maximize the potential search traffic. This strategy also means that a standard five-page website is rarely enough. Your business probably offers a good number of services. If you want to increase the chances of being found in the search engines for numerous sets of keywords, the best way to do that is with numerous pages—one describing each service.

Sample Keyword Map for a Salon and Spa:

Web Page	Keyword Phrase	Development Notes
Home	Happy times day spa Toledo	Be sure to feature your business name and/or the most commonly used search term for the main page, plus city.
Spa Services	Massage therapy Toledo	You may want to feature your leading service for the Services page. Also, this is a good place to provide a brief summary of each additional service with a link to a separate page for each service or group of services.
Facials	Facials Toledo	Get the best results by adding separate pages for individual services.
Spa Facilities	Spa and sauna Toledo	Repeating an important keyword or phrase like "spa" can have the added benefit of keyword concentration across your site.

Page Title

Each and every page on your website should have its own title. The title for each page is displayed at the top of the browser, in the data returned from an internet search, and as the description when the page is bookmarked in someone's internet "favorites" folder. I see a lot of sites that simply read "Home" at the top of the page. Don't make this mistake! Be sure to indicate your business name or a brief description of the page, and incorporate your keywords for that page.

Page Description

Include a brief description for each web page. This is the information that is listed after the page title when your page shows up in search engine results. Make sure your description includes as many of your keywords as possible without being too long. Most search engines will cut off your description after as few as 25 words.

Page Name

The actual name of each web page can also help with placement on Google. For example, the link to the typical "About Us" page might look something like this:

happytimesdayspa.com/aboutus.htm

A keyword-rich link name can be more effective:

happytimesdayspa.com/about-happy-times-day-spa-toledo-ohio.htm

If you are in the process of setting up a new site, you have the opportunity to create keyword-rich links for your pages. If your site is already live, this could be a hassle, but a good web designer can help you make the transition without breaking any existing links on your site.

Example: Happy Times Day Spa Home Page

Home Page Keywords: Happy Times Day Spa Toledo Ohio

Page Title: Happy Times Day Spa in Toledo, Ohio – Massage Therapy, Facials, Waxing

Page Description: Happy Times Day Spa in Toledo, Ohio specializes in massage therapy, facials, and waxing services.

Content: *(keywords are noted in **bold**)*

Welcome to **Happy Times Day Spa,** located in beautiful **Toledo, Ohio**. Our luxurious **day spa** offers everything you need to relax and rejuvenate your senses.

Happy Times Day Spa Services Include:

❖ Massage Therapy – Swedish massage and deep tissue massage.

❖ Facial Treatments and Peels – Designer vitamin facials, anti-aging facials, acne treatment, and microdermabrasion.

❖ Waxing – Body waxing, facial waxing, and bikini waxing.

We invite you to arrive early to take advantage of our distinctive **day spa** facilities. Change into a plush robe and enjoy relaxing in our steam sauna or the hot springs hot tub, which is always set to 110 degrees for maximum detoxification and relaxation.

Happy Times Day Spa is located across from the **Toledo** Mall in the Happy Shopping Center, with plenty of free parking. Our experienced staff is focused on ensuring that you enjoy your **spa** experience and get the relaxation that you need and deserve.

Call **Happy Times Day Spa** today to schedule a **spa** treatment. First-time guests receive 10% off services. 555-555-5555

Incorporating Photos and Video

Photos and videos create visual appeal on your website. From before and after photos and video demonstrations to images of your facilities and staff, there are many ways you can showcase your business and add visual appeal to your website.

Each photo or video that you add to your site not only enhances appeal for the site visitor, but can assist in your SEO strategy. Images have "alt tags," a place where you can include a description of the image for the visually impaired or for visitors who are unable to view images online (some corporations and government entities control employee internet access by blocking images from appearing online). Since the search engines don't yet have the capability of interpreting photo images and video the way that they understand text, they look for the alt image tags and descriptions. Take advantage of the added SEO benefit and make sure that every image you add to your site includes an alt image tag with a keyword-rich description.

Also, including a caption below the photo is yet another opportunity to add a description. Studies also show that site visitors are drawn to reading captions placed below photos. For some reason our eyes are drawn there, and this is an opportunity to bring attention to a key message that you want to convey for that page.

Lastly, the actual file name for each image provides yet another opportunity to improve keyword concentration. For example, instead of inserting an image simply named *photo.jpg*, rename the image to something like *massage-therapy-happy-times-day-spa.jpg*.

Improving Linkability

Links within your website and pointing to your website from other sites can have an important impact on your overall optimization with the search engines.

Inbound Links

One of the criteria that the search engines use to rank website pages is the number of inbound links pointing to your website from other websites. More importantly, they look at how many links from *high-traffic* websites are pointing to your pages. If a popular website features a link to your site, it shows the search engines that your site is relevant.

Other important incoming links are from industry-related sites. When another site in a related industry features a link to your site, it helps Google see your site's relevance. For example, a website that covers news about the spa industry would be an ideal link to have pointing to a salon and spa site.

Government sites (with a .gov extension) and education sites (with a .edu extension) also have high priority with the search engines. If you're able to get incoming links from any of these sites, it can help your ranking.

The key to success here is to make sure your link is listed in as many places as possible.

Where to Promote Your Website Link:

❖ Update the free online profiles provided by any trade organizations that you belong to by including your website link.

❖ Ask colleagues and business partners to swap links with you. They can publish your link on a "Recommended Resources" or similar page on their site, and you can do the same in return.

❖ Publish articles and include your bio and website link. The more articles you push out across the internet, the more links you will have pointing back to your site. The same is true for guest blog posts.

❖ Engage in social media sites, including Facebook, LinkedIn, and Twitter.

❖ Take advantage of every opportunity you can find to post your link online!

Some services offer to add lots of inbound links to your site—beware! Adding dozens of links at once can be viewed by the search engines as spam, and many of these services are scams in their own right.

It takes time to get your link out there, so always be on the lookout for opportunities to add links.

Anchored Links

An anchored link is a link to a web page that is embedded in text. For example, when "Click here for more information" is an active hyperlink to a web page, it is an anchored link.

Anchored links are a boon for SEO because they tell the search engines what content is found on the linked page. Because of this, links should incorporate keywords instead of the generic "Click here" example.

For example, a high-traffic site with a link embedded in the text to "Visit Happy Times Day Spa in Toledo, Ohio" would be an ideal anchored link.

The hardest part of this strategy is getting others to link back to your site in the first place, and then to do so with an anchored link. But because anchored links are so valuable, it's worth your time to ask your link partners to do this whenever possible.

You can also weave anchored links throughout *your own site* to the different pages within your site. For example, from your primary services page, you could include a link that says, "Find out more about massage therapy services." You can also incorporate anchored links on your home page in addition to your site navigation links.

Other Important SEO Strategies

Following are some additional strategies to incorporate into your SEO plans.

Headline Tags

One important factor in featuring the keywords that are central on your web pages is the use of headline tags. A headline is denoted on a web page with basic HTML code: <h1>, <h2>, <h3>, etc. These tags not only affect the formatting of the text, but the search engines interpret headlines as being important content on a page so they should include the keywords for the page. Be sure to check with your web designer to see if your headlines are properly coded. Also note that text in larger fonts or bolded using a <strong> tag will also be noticed by the search engines.

Longevity

Generally speaking, the longer your website is in existence, the better. Newer sites are not regarded as highly by Google as those that have been live for years. There's not much you can do about this, but know that your site's standing will improve over time.

Flash

Flash is technology often used to create dynamic elements on pages (such as rotating images). Some websites have a Flash landing page where you must click to proceed to the site's main page. Unfortunately, Flash is not search-engine-friendly.

Avoid using a Flash introduction page (the main home page for your site) at all costs because it could completely block Google from viewing your site. If you use Flash within your site, be sure to minimize its use and set alt tags that describe the text on the page. It's also a good idea to offer an HTML-only version of your site to help the search engines and to ensure that web users who can't view Flash are still able to view your site.

Broken Links

If you feature links to other websites, be sure to periodically verify that they are working. Google doesn't like broken links, so your ranking can be penalized.

Site Redesign

When you completely redesign your site and upload all of the changes at once, prepare to take a hit from Google. Unfortunately, Google doesn't like it when all of a site's pages change at once, but over time you will regain your position. Also, if you do have your site redesigned, make sure you don't break existing page links. If your page links change or are renamed, ask your web designer to set up .htaccess 301 redirects for each changed link.

XML Sitemap

To help Google crawl all of the pages on your site, ideally you should provide them with a Sitemap. Your website designer should be able to help you with this. If you want to do it yourself, instructions are available here:

http://www.google.com/support/webmasters/bin/answer. py?answer=183668

Content Frequency

I can't emphasize enough the importance of updating website content on a regular basis. One of the worst things you can do is let your website sit idle for weeks or months at a time without adding new content. This tells Google that your site is less relevant than competing sites that are adding content frequently, and thus hurts the ranking of your site.

Ideally, I recommend adding new content to your site a minimum of twice each week, though more is better. The easiest way to do this is with a blog. But you can also add articles, news, videos, and other content. And remember, the more content you add, the more reasons you give Google to find your site. Follow this strategy alone and you are sure to see an increase in the amount of traffic your site receives.

Entrepreneur Interview
Name: John Paul Aguiar

Business name: Money Dummy Blog
Website URL: www.johnpaulaguiar.com
Social media links:

> www.twitter.com/johnaguiar
> www.facebook.com/johnpaulaguiar
> www.facebook.com/moneydummyblog
> https://plus.google.com/102510727932556161605

Tell us about your business and what you do:

I'm a blogger, an internet marketer, and a social media specialist. Lately, focusing more on blog and social media consulting.

I help people set up and build the best blog they can around any niche they have interest in. That includes internet marketing techniques and social media strategies.

The overall goal is to help people make money online, even though I hate to be grouped in with other "MMO" pushers. But reality is that's what I'm here to help people do: make money online.

Who is your target audience?

Honestly, my target audience is anyone who wants to make extra income online. With the economy as bad as it has been, more and more people are coming online to make extra income.

But a more targeted audience for me is small-business owners, bloggers, and marketers. Anyone who is trying to grow a blog or business who needs help with social media, branding, driving traffic, and getting noticed.

How did you get started in your business?

I've been working online for more than 10 years. I had a kidney transplant almost 10 years ago, so I had to look for less structured work; that's what pushed me to look online. I started with a few different MLM opportunities and working social media before it was called social media (ha ha).

I slowly got into internet marketing and learned as much as I could, and then moved into blogging and consulting.

What are some of the best tactics you have used to build your audience and establish your authority online?

It's funny—there are so many things you can do to build your audience and your authority online, and at the same time, it only takes a few things. I guess that's the 80-20 rule in play.

But to build your audience, you first have to have a blog—this is where you can share what you have experience in and share your personality.

Once you have that blog up, you then need to share great content and be YOU—this means be who you are, let your personality shine, and share a little bit about you. People connect with people and stories they can relate to, and no one else can be you.

Next, you need to be on social media sites—as many as you can manage. But at least the Big 5: Twitter, Facebook, LinkedIn, YouTube, and Google+.

Once you're there, you need to work it like your blog: Share great content, be you, be helpful, be available, and connect with people every day.

Next, place yourself everywhere you can, meaning guest post, comment on other blogs, and partner with other people on projects.

If you do all that and stay with it and be consistent, then your audience and authority will grow nicely.

How has social media impacted your business? Any success stories you can share?

The fact that I am now approached for social media consulting and management is a success story. I never planned to offer any services in social media in my business. But because of the success I have had on social media sites, mainly Twitter @JohnAguiar, I have been hired by many people for social media management and consulting, including an up-and-coming pop artist and three book authors.

Social media has helped me explode my blog, business, brand, and friendships, and at the same time opened up a few new income streams.

No matter what you do online, social media DONE CORRECTLY will help you explode your results.

Want more traffic?

Want more readers?

Want more sales?

Want to brand yourself?

Social media will do all this for you, if you are willing to put in the time and work.

Do you engage in any communities and if so, how has that impacted your business?

I visit about three different forums regularly. Anytime you can place yourself into a group of people that are doing the same things as you is always a good idea. At the very least, the friendships you build will be a nice support system.

What role does content play in your marketing strategy?

Content is king—and this is true no matter what you do online.

Content is something you need to develop on a regular basis. The online marketing world has changed since social media has come into play.

If you want to be noticed and stand out, then you need to put out great content daily. Blog posts, videos, articles, and ebooks are good examples.

Your best results will come from using two to three different channels to share your content.

People eat new info differently. Some like to read; some like to watch videos; some like to listen. To better your reach, you need to use all forms of content.

Once you choose a channel, make sure your content is awesome and unique. The best way to build a following is to say things no one else has said before and say it in a way that only you can.

What advice would you offer to readers who want to promote their business online?

I could be here all day with this one, but I'll keep it to this:

Understand that promotion takes work, time, money, and guts to try things others haven't.

Online promotion is no different.

If you have money to spend, then the work you need to put in will be a little less. But it will still be work.

If you are like me when I started, I was broke, so I had to bust my ass and do it all by hand. I had to be creative to find ways to promote that were free and that worked. If this is where you're at, then know it will be hard work and hard work on a daily basis.

The good news is you will fail! You will fail a lot.

Why is that good news?

Because now you know we all failed in the beginning, so you're no different, and knowing that is very freeing.

So put the work in, and if you do that long enough, things do get easier.

If you were starting your business over today, is there anything you would do differently?

I think the only thing I would do differently is I would have gotten into blogging much sooner. Blogging success came much faster six years ago when the competition was much less.

Other than that, I'm pretty happy with the process I took. Some things worked; some things didn't, and I'm OK with that—it has all gotten me to where I am now.

Is there anything else you would like to add?

I touched on this above, but just get out there and do it, no matter what "it" is.

Have a business idea? Then do it. Have a blog idea? Then do it.

Get advice where you can from trusted sources—but at the end of the day, no one knows the future.

No one knows if your idea will work because no one has ever done it, so do it. If it works, great; if not, you will walk away smarter and better off than you were before you failed.

The only way to really fail is to take NO action!

Chapter Six
Blogs Rule

"Every man with an idea has at least two or three followers."
—Brooks Atkinson

I speak on a variety of business topics, but one theme that is included with every presentation that I give is the importance of adding a blog to your site. A blog is hands-down one of the most important elements of a successful website. If you don't yet have one, start by talking with your web developer so that it can be added to your existing site. If you start a blog on another domain, your main site won't reap the traffic benefits. For maximum benefit with the search engines, your blog URL should look like this: *www.yourwebsite.com/blog.*

Depending on the current structure of your website, or if it was built with a template, it may require a complete redesign of your site to incorporate a blog. While this might sound painful, it will be worth it in the long run. A good blog platform to use is www.wordpress. org. If you're not already working with a website designer, ask friends for referrals or consider hiring someone through http://elance.com. Elance is a directory of freelancers, and you can view their portfolios and reviews from others who have used their services.

If you don't yet have a website or need a do-it-yourself option, consider www.typepad.com or www.blogger.com.

How a Blog Benefits Your Business

The Best SEO You Can Get — A blog is essentially an online web diary, making it easy for you to add new content to your site on a regular basis and naturally improving SEO for your site. Remember, Google likes fresh content. The more you add to your blog, the more Google will pay attention. And each new post gives Google another reason to find your site, which ultimately increases traffic.

Syndication – Blogs contain technology called Really Simple Syndication (RSS), which allows users to easily monitor your content by subscribing to your feed. This makes it easy for prospects to follow your new posts and essentially turns your blog into an online magazine of sorts. Note: Make sure your RSS feed link is easy to find on your site. I've seen too many sites make the mistake of not including this link in prime real estate. When it comes to doing anything online, make it as easy as possible for visitors!

Visitor Engagement – A blog enhances the community focus because site visitors can leave comments on your blog, ask questions, and interact with you.

Impress Prospects – The more content you can provide your site visitors, the more likely they will be to call you. Andrew Rogerson is a business broker who has filled his website (http://www.rogersonbusinessservices.com/) with content. If I were getting ready to sell my business and found his site, I would be beyond impressed. He offers all kinds of helpful articles and tips for preparing a business for sale, purchasing a business, purchasing a franchise, and more. His content gives you a sense of who he is and the authority he has in his field. Incidentally, he's also an author of several books and is utilizing many of the strategies in this book. It's no surprise that when I searched Google for "Sacramento business broker"—a highly competitive search phrase—his site comes up in the number one position.

The Heart of Your Social Media Strategy – If you're going to get involved with Facebook, Twitter, or LinkedIn, a blog is essential. Each new blog post should be shared with your social media networks, linking readers back to your site.

Media and Other Opportunities – When you use the strategies outlined in this book, establish your authority in your field, and then develop compelling blog posts, all kinds of opportunities can come your way. Media professionals frequently use Google to find sources, and when you write about topics that they're looking for, and you're blogging on a regular basis, there's a good chance they will find you. This has happened to me more times than I can count—really!

Developing Blog Content

Blogging can feel a bit overwhelming when you're just getting started. You may wonder what to write about, how you're going to find the time, and how you're going to keep it up. I've been there myself! Early on, I went through a period of "bloggers block" where I just didn't have any ideas that I felt worked for the blog. I took an extended break and regrouped before returning and finding my groove.

As for how often you should update your blog, that depends on your goals. In the world according to Google, the more content the better. As I've mentioned earlier, I usually recommend a minimum of two to three times per week. If that scares you, start with one! Hopefully, you'll find that you actually enjoy blogging and it won't feel like work.

Following are some tips that have helped me keep it going through the years.

1. **Keep a notepad with you at all times.** I find that the best blog ideas come to me in the car, while on a walk, standing in line at Starbucks, or while cleaning out a closet. I also know that I can forget an idea as quickly as it came to me, so I've developed the habit of writing them down immediately.

2. **Develop a system.** Take those ideas on scrap paper and sticky notes and keep an "idea journal" on your desk. You may not want to write about each idea immediately. Some should

simmer for a bit. Keep a list so you can always find an idea to cover in a pinch, or so you can revisit ideas later on.

3. **Read online daily.** Reading other blogs and news sites can spark endless ideas. You might want to expand on a topic another blogger covers and link back to that blog as a point of reference. You might want to voice a contrary opinion. You may come across a new industry report or statistic that begs to be written about. To develop great content, not to mention learn something new, read daily.

4. **Keep it short and sweet.** Blog posts don't need to be full-length articles. A single paragraph with a quick tip or a link to a favorite resource can do just fine. Mix it up by writing shorter and longer posts. If a post becomes really long, break it up into a series and mark them "Part 1," Part 2," "Part 3," etc.

5. **Step away from your desk.** These days I rarely get writer's block, but when I'm struggling to write something and it isn't flowing easily, then I know I need to get away from it for awhile. Take a walk, focus on another task, or grab some coffee. Don't force it. Come back to it when you're ready.

6. **Don't be afraid to move on.** Sometimes a blog post just doesn't flow. Instead of agonizing over it, save your work and start something else. I can't tell you how often I start to write a post and then decide to save it and write something else. Usually, a week or even a month later I decide I'm ready to tackle it again and cross the finish line.

7. **Develop lists.** Readers love numbered lists, which is why you see headlines on most magazines that read "8 Ways to Save Money" or "7 Signs Your Marriage Needs a Boost." I write a lot of lists and not just because they are popular with readers; I find them easier to write. What I'm writing now is a list. But lists don't need to consist of full paragraphs. You can also list resources, book recommendations, technology tips, favorite tweeters, and much more.

8. **Flex your muscle.** Writing involves a muscle in your brain that must be exercised regularly. Just like workouts at the gym, the more you do it, the easier it gets.

9. **Don't edit while you write.** This is the secret that most writers live by. Instead of re-reading over sentences you just wrote and critiquing every line, write first and edit later. Let the ideas flow.

10. **Post excerpts from your books and products.** If you've authored a book or written a special report or ebook, share occasional excerpts on your blog. As a bonus, these can spark product sales.

11. **Invite guest bloggers.** Ask your peers, clients, and website visitors to contribute articles for your blog. Create some basic guidelines and periodically remind them about the opportunity.

12. **Peruse your bookshelf.** Some writers find casual reading loosens things up (like fiber for the mind!). Read a chapter in an unrelated book or flip through a magazine. Once you've cleared the cobwebs, try again.

13. **Write in Word first.** Sometimes when I start writing a post directly in my WordPress control panel, I freeze. I feel pressured by some non-existent time limit. Writing first in Microsoft Word releases some of that pressure, not to mention the help of the good old spell-check feature.

14. **Shoot your inner perfectionist.** I'm a perfectionist at heart and can be my own worst enemy. I've learned to let it go when it comes to blogging. I find the occasional misspelling or typo in my work. Oh well, life goes on.

15. **Mix it up.** Your blog doesn't have to consist solely of articles and stories. Mix it up by adding videos, podcasts, interviews, photos, or even a funny cartoon (provided you get permission if it's someone else's work).

16. **Write ahead.** When the mood strikes or you can plan some extra time in your schedule, write as many blog posts as you

can at once. Then you can schedule them to publish at different intervals during the coming week.

17. **Find your groove.** I used to be a night owl before I was a mom, but these days I find my most productive hours are early in the morning. Most days, I try to write a blog post or two before I even open email. I also find that the world does not come to an end as a result of checking email later in the day.

18. **Designate brainstorming time.** Once in awhile, usually when I'm traveling or sitting in a coffee shop, I challenge myself to brainstorm blog topics and let them fly. On a good day, I can wrangle 20 or 30 ideas on a page in just 15 minutes. Some topics ultimately end up getting combined, some thrown out, and some become some of my best content.

19. **Write when it hits you.** Sometimes you may just get inspired to write something in the middle of the day. This happens to me all the time and often results in some of my best work. If the mood strikes and you can make the time, go with it!

20. **Make it a habit.** You've probably heard that it takes 21 days to develop a habit. What if you challenged yourself to blog every day for three weeks? Do you think the sky would fall? Do you think you'd end up in the fetal position? Or do you think it might get easier and maybe even feel like an accomplishment? I bet you'll be surprised by the results.

21. **Never forget your target audience.** Your content should be all about appealing to the people you most want to reach. What is interesting to you may not be interesting to your audience, so be very clear about their interests and needs.

22. **Have fun with it.** With any luck you will find that blogging can be a fun creative outlet. I see a lot of resistance from people when I tell them to blog, often because it sounds like a lot of work, requires time, and puts you in the spotlight. But if you can overcome these mental hurdles, develop your content with authenticity, and serve your audience, you might

actually find that it becomes something you enjoy. Updating my blog has become one of my favorite things I do each week.

If you find that you simply hate it, then by all means hire someone to help make it happen.

Blog Promotion Strategies

The fact is that it takes time to build blog readership, though sometimes a topic just takes off. For a good example, rent the movie *Julie and Julia*, which is based on the true story of Julie Powell's adventures in cooking Julia Child's recipes over the course of a year. Powell began blogging about her cooking efforts and it quickly caught on. Blog traffic grew rapidly and she eventually ended up with a book deal and a major motion picture.

Unfortunately, most blogs don't hit the media jackpot like Powell's did, but the point is that it can happen. To give your blog an extra boost, following are some promotion strategies.

❖ Announce your blog posts to your social media networks on a regular basis, including post title and a link back to the post (to drive traffic!).

❖ Share your blog link on all online profiles, such as in your Facebook bio or your member profile with your trade association.

❖ Share blog posts and links in your e-newsletter.

❖ Write about specific people or businesses and then send them a link to the post. Encourage them to share with their networks.

❖ Invite others to submit guest blog posts. Most will be inclined to share their post with their networks.

❖ Use your blog as a launch point for contests and special promotions. Conduct campaigns that inspire readers to share with their networks.

❖ Blog often. More is better when it comes to content online.

❖ Pay attention to which posts get the most attention, and which ones fall flat. They can't all be winners. Notice when you get the most comments so that you can do more of what works.

❖ Invite people to respond. A very small percentage of site visitors actually take the time to comment on your blog. However, you can increase results by asking a question that urges readers to respond.

❖ Participate in blog carnivals. A blog carnival is essentially a roundup of blog posts from various sites based on a specific topic. The blog host benefits from featuring other people's blog posts because contributors often share the link with their networks, and contributors benefit from exposure with the host's audience plus a link back to the contributor's site. Join http://blogcarnival.com to find a list of bloggers seeking posts for upcoming carnivals.

❖ Submit your blog link to blog directories for greater exposure. Here's a list:

- http://blogcatalog.com
- http://mybloglog.com
- http://blogflux.com
- http://technorati.com
- http://blogarama.com
- http://blogexplosion.com
- http://bloghub.com
- http://globeofblogs.com
- http://networkedblogs.com
- http://bloghop.com

RSS Feeds

As mentioned earlier, blogs feature technology called Really Simple Syndication (RSS). This makes it easy for other people to follow and read new posts from your blog, which is one of the many reasons why blogs are so important and powerful. This is accomplished using an RSS reader such as Google Reader (http://google.com/reader). Once you set up a reader account, when you click on an RSS feed for a blog, it is saved to your reader and automatically updated there. This essentially creates a sort of news feed so that users can easily scan and read blog posts from their favorite sites.

If you're not familiar with this technology, go set up a reader account and then find some blogs to follow so you can better understand how it all works.

For your own blog, you will want to be able to monitor how many users subscribe to your RSS feed. One great service that can do this for you is http://feedburner.com. Follow the instructions to set up your account and then log in periodically to check your stats.

Entrepreneur Interview
Name: Shasta Nelson

Business name: GirlFriendCircles.com
Website URL: www.girlfriendcircles.com

Social Media Links:

> http://www.facebook.com/girlfriendcircles
> http://twitter.com/#!/girlfrndcircles
> http://www.girlfriendcircles.com/blog/

Tell us about your business and what you do:

GirlFriendCircles.com is a women's friendship matching site. My website provides online tools for women to meet new local friends offline. As CEO, I oversee the operations, marketing, and community interaction. My favorite part is writing and speaking on the subject of friendships, normalizing the need for new friends, and giving guidelines that help ensure healthy expectations.

Who is your target audience?

Women 21-65 who live in/near a major city, know the value of friendship, and prefer small group conversations over large networking events. Most of our members have recently experienced a life change (move to new city, divorce, empty-nest), or come up for air from work, a relationship, or their kids and realize that their friendships have drifted away.

How did you get started in your business?

While working as a life coach, I found that my clients could line up three dates for next weekend easier than they could find female friendship. With life transitions causing women to replace half their friends every seven years, the need couldn't be more obvious. And with more of us working from home and going through life stages at various ages, I knew we needed more ways to match up women who know the value of female friendship. It's simply too awkward to go hit on women for friendship. I kept looking for resources for them only to discover that everything was either big local networking events where you had to shake hands and mingle, or up to the women themselves to set up the possibly uncomfortable one-on-one friend date. I decided to start matching women who valued fostering new friends into local groups to meet.

What are some of the best tactics you have used to build your audience and establish your authority online?

I'm a big fan of people leaning into their strengths—no one person can do every option out there. For me, blogging and writing was my passion and it also helped me establish a voice of expertise on the subject. Having others feature my blogs or link to them helped grow my audience. And turning some of those blogs into media pitches for TV interviews helped me grow my credibility. I'd also say that my involvement in Facebook and Twitter has been significant in helping me network with influencers—primarily Twitter, as it has allowed me to find and partner with women who can introduce my business to their audiences.

How has social media impacted your business? Any success stories you can share?

One of my most significant Twitter stories is from a couple of years ago when I started following a few people who were talking about women's friendship—a psychologist-author, two women who ran an online girls' night out idea site, a blogger who was telling stories of her own search for new friends, etc. In connecting with them individually, we all started e-introducing each other, and promoting each other. Eventually, someone suggested we officially commit to a causal alliance, and we formed the Friendship Circle. Over time, we've featured each other's blogs, interviewed each other, re-tweeted important announcements, worked together for Women's Friendship Month, and pitched each other for publicity opportunities. It feels so good to be connected to others who share my passion for the cause, and we all know that we're all more successful when we work together. Without Twitter, we wouldn't have even found each other or had easy ways to start helping each other.

Do you engage in any communities and if so, how has that impacted your business?

Absolutely. I'm a part of the San Francisco Coaches Association that meets monthly—they provide me ongoing training, brainstorming ideas, and contacts. I also participated this year in a monthly mastermind group of female entrepreneurs, which was super meaningful. I don't network to sell my services—that's all online. I network to keep myself stimulated with new ideas and support. And, of course, everyone I meet now has the potential of telling others about my services if they know someone who might need new friends.

What role does content play in your marketing strategy?

For me, content is everything. I'd have long given up on the business if I weren't so passionate about the content. Someone once told me a business has to initially decide to either go the PR route or the advertising route—both can feel risky and expensive. For me, because I love teaching and inspiring action, I chose the PR route so I could share my content. I blog for *The Huffington Post*, contribute guest posts for selected blogs, and teach on YouTube video blogs. It has taken a lot of time to grow the credibility and expertise necessary, though. This is not a game for those looking for immediate results. Content has to ultimately come from a place where you're doing it because you love it and know it better than others.

What advice would you offer to readers who want to promote their business online?

Find the websites where your target market hangs out and figure out how to connect with them. Connect with them in whatever way works best for you—sponsor a contest with them by donating your product/service as a prize, offer to guest blog, comment on their blogs, offer to interview them on your website/blog (they'll likely share the interview with their audience), pay for an ad on their site, ask them what you can do that would help them the most (some people just want traffic to their site, whereas others would prefer you promote their ebook). Basically, do what you can to give value to what they're doing. They will reciprocate when there is trust and opportunity.

If you were starting your business over today, is there anything you would do differently?

Because most women don't know that a resource like this exists, I wish I had known more about SEO to help me get in front of them on Google searches. Also, though impossible, I wish I had known how to set up the website perfectly the first time—I can't believe how many times we have made, and will continue to make, fundamental changes. But perhaps the biggest wish I had, and still do have, is figuring out more strategic ways I could maximize the role that local ambassadors can provide. Online is important, no doubt about it. But for me, having local women care enough to get involved in tangible ways would have made a significant difference!

Quick Tip

BusinessInfoGuide.com features interviews with entrepreneurs and authors, which are featured on the home page of the site and promoted via social media. This also adds a link back to your site and exposure to site visitors. To contribute, simply fill out the online form.

http://businessinfoguide.com/directory/ contribute/

Chapter Seven
Social Media Simplified

"Each friend represents a world in us,
a world possibly not born until they arrive,
and it is only by this meeting that a new world is born."
—Anais Nin

Though I've been marketing online since 2003, like a lot of people, I was initially resistant to the social media frenzy. I was already too busy and didn't want to get involved in anything else that would potentially take up any more of my time. But once I started to investigate the possibilities, I quickly discovered the power that exists in social media.

This chapter focuses on The Big Three: Facebook, LinkedIn, and Twitter. These are currently the most active social networks for business, and each brings its own unique value. Also worth noting is Google Plus, which has recently entered the scene. We will talk about that, too.

How Social Media Can Benefit Your Business

In a nutshell, social media allows you to connect, communicate, and share compelling content with your target audience. All of the major social media sites provide the opportunity to search for users by keyword (e.g., by city or industry). It's relatively easy to find your potential clients. The real challenge is in keeping them engaged.

As the newspaper industry continues to suffer a slow death, social media has become a resource for information. News on social networks can break and spread at lightning speed. I personally learned about the deaths of Michael Jackson and Ted Kennedy through the almost instantaneous posts on Twitter.

During the wildfires in Southern California in 2008, the firefighters posted updates from the scene on Twitter. Many would argue that Barack Obama won the presidential election largely due to the viral marketing campaigns launched through social media sites.

It is almost frightening to think about the power that social media holds and how it is shaping our world.

Think social media is a waste of time? Here are some ways it can impact your business:

- ❖ Build brand recognition
- ❖ Change brand perception
- ❖ Establish or showcase expertise in your field
- ❖ Attract new clients
- ❖ Generate repeat exposure with existing clients and prospects
- ❖ Promote products
- ❖ Promote services
- ❖ Promote events
- ❖ Reach your local community
- ❖ Reach the global community
- ❖ Set your business apart from competitors
- ❖ Create leverage for media opportunities, publishing contracts, corporate sponsorships, speaking engagements, and more (a large network creates demand)
- ❖ Trigger a viral effect

Viral Marketing Defined

When someone is compelled to share your message (forward an email, video clip, or some other form of electronic communication) and that is replicated repeatedly, the message takes on a viral effect. When used for marketing purposes, a viral campaign can be incredibly powerful.

One example of viral marketing comes from Blendtec's "Will It Blend?" campaign. To demonstrate the power of its blenders, the company began featuring videos on YouTube where they blended all kinds of crazy items: a lit, full-sized tiki torch, a camera, 53 toy cars, and even an iPad. Viewers couldn't help but pass those videos along to friends, making them an internet sensation.

Viral campaigns are online marketing gold, though they aren't easy to manufacture. The hope is that with social media, you'll create something compelling enough that others pass it along quickly.

What to Share on Social Media:

❖ Your new blog posts with a link to the post

❖ Someone else's blog post

❖ An article you've written

❖ An article from somewhere else

❖ A video demonstration

❖ A funny or controversial video

❖ Before and after photos of work you've done

❖ Humorous or inspiring photos

❖ Client success stories/case studies

❖ Free ebook

❖ Special report

❖ White paper

❖ Upcoming event announcement

❖ Live reports from an event you are currently attending

❖ Book reviews/recommendations

❖ Recommended products

❖ Recommended services

❖ Tips for doing something better

❖ How-to suggestions

❖ A series of related posts

❖ Recent media coverage you have received

❖ Inspirational advice (preferably your own—motivational quotes are overused online)

❖ Forward someone else's update (with proper credit attribution)

❖ Breaking news alerts

❖ Leads for opportunities (media, clients, etc.)

❖ Requests for participation (guest posts on your blog, speaker for an event you're hosting, etc.)

❖ Interesting photo from a recent event

❖ Teleseminar/webinar invitation

❖ Contest announcements

❖ Special sales, offers, and discounts (delivered sparingly)

❖ Request for audience feedback

❖ A compelling question you want answered

❖ Anything offered for free

❖ Insider tips that people won't find anywhere else

❖ Your opinion on just about anything with target audience appeal

What NOT to Share on Social Media

❖ Information about when you're heading out on vacation or other personal information that strangers could take advantage of. There have been reports of robberies conducted due to social media announcements like these, so be careful.

❖ Too much personal information about your family, birthdates, where your kids go to school, or other details that could be a target for identity thieves or creepy people. Social media is public, so be smart about what you share and don't share.

❖ Negative or derogatory remarks about people or brands. Be careful about what you say as you could end up in a lawsuit; plus, it just doesn't look very nice and can turn off your audience.

❖ Motivational quotes. Okay, this won't break any laws, and it mostly falls under my list of personal pet peeves. Quotes are entirely overused on social media and don't do anything to set your business apart or claim your authority in your field. Try to come up with more interesting content!

Facebook Basics

One of the biggest benefits that social media platforms like Facebook provide the business community is the ability to get repeat exposure with the people in your network. Clients, peers, and prospects can make up your network, and you can promote events, sales, special offers, and more through your Facebook profile.

Not only is Facebook a tool for your business, it can be a fun way to connect with old friends, family, and coworkers. There is something about sharing an old grade school photo that can create an instant bond with those from your past. And keep in mind that even personal connections have the potential to become new clients and business alliances.

How it Works

Facebook was initially designed to function like an interactive online yearbook. You start by creating a free personal profile that includes a photo and some biographical information. Next, you can search for people you know and send them friend requests. Once accepted, your friends can see your profile and updates and you can see theirs.

Central to the whole system is the status update box on Facebook that asks, "What's on your mind?" Here is where users can share brief updates about anything from what they had for lunch to where they are headed for their next meeting.

These status updates make up a running stream of content. When you view your home page on Facebook, you will see a news feed of the status updates from those you are connected to. In addition to brief text-based messages, users can share photos, videos, and links. It's a bit like being a voyeur into the lives of those you're connected to. You also have the opportunity to comment back on a friend's post and begin to engage in online conversation.

Using Facebook for Business

When leveraging Facebook for business, instead of sharing mundane details like the flavor of your latte of the day or which kid has the flu, you can share details about your business. For example, you might share a link to a recent blog post or a link to an industry news article.

Though these details may not matter much to your family and friends, they will matter to your customers and prospects. This is where things start to get interesting. As you build a following of people in your community, you have an opportunity to engage them in your business.

Ready to get started? Here are some ways to maximize Facebook:

Start with a Personal Profile

There is no cost to create a profile on Facebook and based on site policies, your profile must be tied to a human name, not a business name. Do yourself a favor and keep your personal profile personal. Early on I used my personal profile for business, which has several limitations. Personal profiles are only allowed up to 5,000 friends, so I've been maxed out for some time. They also aren't visible on a Google search. A better bet is to use your personal profile to get familiar with how Facebook works, connect with your friends and family, and then launch a fan page for your business.

Create a Fan Page

Facebook offers free business profiles known as pages, of which followers can become fans. You can create a fan page for a business, product, book, author, speaker, celebrity or just about anything you want. To create a page, from your Facebook home page click on "Pages" in the left sidebar. You will find some helpful explanations about how pages work, along with a link that will allow you to create your page.

Pages function a lot like profiles so you can add links, events, applications, and other features that make them interactive. The big difference is that instead of sending friend requests like you do with a personal profile, users must become fans of your page by clicking on the Like button.

Once a user likes your page, he will see your updates in his Facebook news feed. Like everything else you do online, share great content. Ask questions and respond to any posts added by visitors to your page.

Facebook Groups

Online groups allow you to network virtually with potential clients and peers. To access groups, start from your Facebook home page and click on "Groups." You can browse through thousands of themed groups with topics ranging from business to politics and everything in between.

You can search groups by city name, theme, or any type of keyword. Start by searching for nearby cities. Business-related groups are a good place to focus since you're representing a business and can connect with other business-minded people. If you really want to maximize the potential with groups, consider starting one of your own.

Involve Your Staff

Your staff members can bring added exposure for your business on Facebook, though a word of caution here: you don't want them to do more harm than good! If you have young people working for you who use their Facebook pages to share drunken college photos, you probably don't want them talking about your business. But if you have staff members who want to build their business networks, by all means help them extend the reach of your business. Either way, social media warrants a conversation with your staff to educate them on the DOs and DON'Ts.

Facebook Engagement Tips

❖ Post new content daily, though only if you have something interesting to share! Posting for the sake of posting won't inspire your audience.

❖ Never forget your niche audience. Everything you do should speak to their needs, challenges, and desires.

❖ Be a resource. Share great content, whether your own or content from others. The point is to give value.

❖ When you write a new blog post, share the title and a link back to your site on your page to bring traffic directly to your website.

❖ Use photos often since these get extra visibility on Facebook. Get creative! For example, if you're a hair stylist, ask your clients if you can snap a photo of their fresh new style and then tag them on Facebook. This makes the photo available to each of your clients' networks, too. Do the same thing with events that you hold or any other opportunity you can create to capture people on film.

❖ Videos also tend to get added visibility, so post them liberally.

❖ Respond to each person who leaves a comment on your page. Let the person know you're listening and show appreciation. If someone asks a question about your business, respond directly on the page so others can see the answer. This is part of building your community.

❖ Be funny, smart, engaging, or even controversial if it appeals to your audience.

❖ Like other people's pages. Make sure you aren't simply operating in broadcast mode.

❖ Ask questions and invite your audience to contribute to your page.

❖ Consider holding a live chat event on your page where users can come ask you questions and get answers immediately. Note that this will take some pre-promotion effort to ensure you get a good turnout.

❖ Know that it takes time to find your "voice" and build momentum. Stick a toe in the Facebook waters and start experimenting. Pay attention to what people respond to.

❖ Building a following requires ongoing effort. If you use LinkedIn and Twitter, cross-promote with your following on those sites and invite them to come on over to your Facebook page.

❖ Post your Facebook link (and all of your social media links) on the home page or sidebar of your website.

Twitter Basics

Twitter is a microblogging platform and is built around status updates (similar to those on Facebook). The biggest difference is that Twitter only allows you to post 140 characters at a time—about one sentence. This forces your communication to be concise, to say the least.

Twitter profiles are also much simpler than the profiles on Facebook. You have just a few sentences to describe who you are, along with a link to your website. For users to view your posts, they must choose to "Follow" you, similar to the "Like" button on Facebook. Once they follow you, your posts will appear in their news feeds.

Know the Terminology

Twitter has a language all its own. Here's a brief overview:

Tweet: A message of up to 140 characters you post as your status update for your followers to see.

Twitter handle: Your Twitter username is also known as your handle. An "at" symbol (@) always precedes a Twitter handle, which makes it clickable on Twitter. For example, my Twitter handle is @bizauthor, so anyone who wants to send me a direct tweet would begin the message with my handle.

Retweet, aka RT: When you forward a tweet from someone else to your followers, this is known as a retweet and should begin with RT so that followers know what you're doing:

RT @bizauthor: How to create a media sheet for radio interviews http://ow.ly/5NSIF

Direct Message, aka DM: This is a direct message that you send to someone's Twitter inbox, which is the equivalent of email on Twitter.

Hashtag: Placing a hashtag (also known as a pound sign, "#") in front of a word improves the word's track-ability in Twitter search and makes it clickable. For example, if you are giving away a free report, you might include #freereport in your tweet so that you can easily search to find posts with this reference. Hashtags are also useful for helping your content show up when people search. For example, if your post is tagged with #technology, anyone searching for that key phrase can view it (which can bring you new followers!).

Create a Twitter Account

For your company Twitter handle, use your personal name, business name, or some version of it if available. Though it's possible to change your handle down the road, it may confuse your audience, so be thoughtful with this initial decision.

Set Up Your Profile

Write an interesting business description and include your website link and a logo or photo of your business. It's also a good branding strategy to set a unique background (wallpaper) for your profile. Many graphic designers create custom Twitter backgrounds for around $100, and this is a worthy investment to make a distinctive impression.

Start Following People You Know

To begin getting comfortable with Twitter, start following others. Search for people you know or authors that you admire. Sit back and watch what others are doing and then begin to join in. You can search Twitter by name or keywords (http://search.twitter.com/). Also search for people through directories like http://Twellow.com and http://wefollow.com.

Another reason to follow others is that they may take time to view your profile and learn more about you. Not all will, especially if they have a large volume of followers to keep up with. But many do. Last year, I came across a list of media pros on Twitter and decided to follow those who covered business. Sure enough, within a few weeks one of them contacted me and interviewed me for a story.

Pay Attention to Posts

Are you finding interesting articles and valuable information? From a marketing perspective, this is the greatest advantage of using Twitter. You can exchange useful information with those who follow you, and learn from those who you are following. This is also a great way to learn how people are using Twitter successfully. Pay attention to what you like and don't like about how others are sharing information on Twitter.

Share Useful Information

Twitter was designed as a tool to share what you are up to. While you can tweet about what you're having for lunch, it's really not relevant (and can be annoying). As with other forms of social media, there is an abundance of "noise" like this on Twitter, so if you want to stand out, share useful content, respond to your audience, and be interesting. You want to be a resource for your followers so that they will pay attention to what you're up to and want to learn more.

Engage With Your Audience

When you share something interesting, others will click your link, retweet your post, or reply back to you. Look for opportunities to engage in conversation. Reply to people whose posts you find interesting. Retweet other people's posts often, as your followers will appreciate useful information and those whose posts you share will be grateful. The more you engage the more benefits you will see as a result.

Be Interesting!

Let your personality shine through. Humor is always a good way to attract people. Find ways to stand out from the crowd.

Monitor Activity on Twitter

If you follow a lot of people on Twitter, your news feeds are going to be very active. Because I follow back all of my followers, I see updates from thousands of people, which makes it impossible to see everything or to keep track of the people and businesses whose tweets I enjoy most.

Because of this, there are several Twitter tools available to help with monitoring. The one I like most is TweetDeck, which is free and can be downloaded at http://tweetdeck.com. TweetDeck displays columns where you can create lists to better monitor Twitter activity. For example, I have a column for "Favorites" where tweets appear from the people I've chosen for that list. I also have columns that search for keywords, such as my website URL and my name, allowing me to monitor when these are mentioned.

TweetDeck makes it easy to reply and retweet right from the console. You can also display a column with "Mentions" that displays tweets that include your Twitter handle. This is a great way to monitor how many people are retweeting your content or mentioning you. I also find that TweetDeck helps tremendously with social media time management. I keep it open on my desktop at all times so I can quickly hop on and view the latest updates when I have a few minutes to spare.

TweetDeck isn't the only option for better Twitter monitoring. HootSuite (http://hootsuite.com) offers similar features.

Schedule and Repeat Your Tweets

Because most of us don't spend all day on Twitter (we have work to do, right?), we only see tweets that are currently displaying at the time we log in. Because of this, when it comes to sharing content, it's a good idea to tweet it out more than once.

Yes, social media is about connecting with your audience, but Twitter in particular is a powerful platform for sharing content. When I log in to view the feeds of the people and businesses I follow on Twitter, I'm not interested in who's chatting with each other or what the weather looks like today. I'm looking for interesting content. Show me a link to a blog with something new to think about or a breaking news story.

In fact, you could argue that anyone who uses Twitter regularly is actually a publisher. And because I maintain two blogs, I am keenly aware of the opportunity to share my latest posts on Twitter. Not everyone in my following is going to see when I've added a new post. But if I post it again–and again and again–there's a better chance it will be seen.

So my strategy is simple. When I write a new blog post, I share it immediately. Then I log in to HootSuite (http://hootsuite.com) and schedule it to post again within a day or two. And then again the following week. And then again a week later. In fact, for each new blog post I will often schedule it to post from six to twenty times over the next three months.

Quite frankly, I wish more people did this because I know I miss a lot of great content on Twitter, and I can't afford to spend a whole day monitoring the site. I have to hop on and view new posts in between calls, appointments, and projects, which is how most people use Twitter.

Also, to make it easier to manage my posts, I created a simple Twitter Schedule. I check off the boxes under the dates and times as I schedule a post to go out. You can download a free copy of my Twitter

Schedule form here: http://businessinfoguide.com/wp-content/uploads/Twitter-Schedule-Templates.pdf.

The bottom line: tweet and repeat. This is not about automating all of your tweets. You should absolutely still get involved, engage, and retweet other relevant content. But you can also take advantage of this powerful publishing platform and get your content seen.

Tweet Old Post

If your blog is built in Wordpress and you have a lot of content in your archives, one great plugin you should add is Tweet Old Post (http://wordpress.org/extend/plugins/tweet-old-post/). This handy tool automates the sharing of your old blog posts based on the interval you set, which is typically every one to four hours. This ensures that you are posting content to Twitter around the clock and getting visibility for the great content you previously created. This plugin has generated a tremendous amount of traffic, blog comments, and retweets for my old posts so I highly recommend it for your Wordpress blog.

Shrink Your Links

Because of the limited space to share information on Twitter, a great option is to use a link-shortening service such as http://bit.ly/. This free tool will also track how many click-throughs your link received. So if you want to link to a new blog post, you can shorten the URL to save space and then track the results and find out how many people clicked the link. Pay attention to the trends so you know how your audience is responding to your posts.

Follow Back

The process of following someone on Twitter is a one-way activity. If I choose to follow someone, that person is not required to follow me back. Whether or not to follow users back on Twitter has been a subject of much debate. Here are some reasons why I believe it's a good strategy.

1. **Let Them Know You're Paying Attention**
   When someone chooses to follow you, they are interested in what you have to say. The hope is that many of your followers will become customers. With that in mind, following them back shows you're paying attention. It shifts your business

from broadcast mode on Twitter to a company that values its followers enough to pay attention.

For a great example, see @Comcastcares. As a cable provider, Comcast has improved its overall customer service ratings by following its customers back and responding to their questions and concerns directly on Twitter. This effort has shifted the perception about the company's service and helped them to build a more loyal customer base.

2. **Provide Social Currency**
   A follow on Twitter is a form of social currency. When someone follows you, you can repay the favor by following back. Everyone wants more followers on Twitter, so the simple gesture of following back is a great way to show your thanks to those who follow you.

3. **Learn About Your Followers**
   By following back, you receive a window into the conversations of your potential customers. You can learn what they are concerned about and what interests them. This can become valuable market research.

4. **Support Your Followers**
   Start retweeting and acknowledging posts by your followers and you can build loyalty and personal connections with them.

5. **Gain More Followers**
   Twitter places limits on how many people you can follow if you aren't building your own following. That means that a user with 100 followers cannot follow 5,000 companies. Each users needs to be building a following, too. When you follow back, you increase your chances of users choosing to follow you because they will know you are reciprocating.

6. **Manage the Masses**
   I've heard the argument that if you follow everyone back you can end up with thousands of people to follow, which can make your Twitter news feed look like it's on overdrive. Yes, thousands of followers can be a lot to manage, but you

can simplify the process by using a tool like TweetDeck to create a list of favorite people to follow. This makes it easy to monitor the news from those who you want to stay close to, and still allows you to pop over and look at your full news feed when time permits.

7. **Save Time by Automating**

   Though it would be nice to view the profiles of every follower, it's not realistic when your Twitter following climbs into the thousands. The good news is that you don't have to manually follow each new follower; you can automate the follow-back process with the free service from http://socialoomph.com.

8. **Manage Spammers (it's not as bad as you think)**

   If you follow everyone back, you will inevitably encounter spammers. That's a small price to pay when growing your network, and there is a surprisingly simple way to deal with this. Drum roll, please … All you need to do is delete them! If you use TweetDeck to manage your Twitter activity, you can easily click a button to block and report spam. You can also locate spammers when reading your full news feed and simply remove them. I can tell you from experience that this isn't an overwhelming or a time-consuming problem.

Twitter Engagement Tips

❖ Twitter news feeds move quickly when you're following a lot of people. That means that when you share a new post, it is only likely being seen by a fraction of your following—those who happen to be viewing Twitter around the same time. Because of this, I recommend repeating tweets. Remember, Twitter is a platform for content so repeating interesting posts actually benefits you and your audience.

❖ Get in the habit of scheduling posts on Twitter. Dig into your archives and share previous blog posts! Just don't automate everything; you still need to have a human presence there.

❖ Share new content on Twitter as often as possible. Ideally, I'd recommend a minimum of six times per day—though more is better. Again, not everyone is on Twitter at the same time. The more often you post, the better your chances of being seen by your audience.

- ❖ Leave room for others to retweet your posts. As much as possible, keep your posts to 120 characters or less; otherwise, it's harder to forward along.

- ❖ Follow those who follow you.

- ❖ Respond to those who reach out to you or share your content. Get involved.

- ❖ Retweet often. Forwarding someone else's content along benefits your audience and the person you've just featured.

- ❖ Fall in love with Twitter. I personally love it because I learn a lot from following people and companies on Twitter that share content I'm interested in. It's a pleasure to log on many times each day to see what's new. Once you really start to enjoy it, you will begin to find your groove and your following will grow as a result.

LinkedIn Basics

LinkedIn is a business-focused network. The vast majority of users here are using LinkedIn for some kind of business networking purpose such as job hunting, marketing, or sales. It's a smaller network compared to the mammoth Facebook, but it's highly targeted for reaching professionals who can afford your services.

Your LinkedIn profile can read more like a résumé as you can include work history along with website and social media links. Be sure to have keywords in mind when writing your LinkedIn profile. It should have a solid description of your business and what you do. Keywords can help others find you when they search for related keywords. I have received many business opportunities as a direct result of filling out my profile as completely as possible.

When you send a connection request to users on LinkedIn, you are required to know them or be acquainted with them in some way. It's harder to build a large following here because you will need to know the person's email address or be members of the same group on LinkedIn to connect. You can also import your contacts into LinkedIn to easily locate the people you know.

With LinkedIn, you can share status updates just like you do on Facebook and Twitter. You can also ask people to write a testimonial for you, which will be publicly visible.

You can also search LinkedIn for names or keywords. If you would like to connect with someone you don't know, look to see if you have any connections in common. If so, you can ask to be introduced. Some business owners use this method to generate leads and reach out to new contacts. If you don't share a common connection, you can upgrade to a paid LinkedIn account and gain the ability to send a limited number of LinkedIn mail messages to contacts outside of your network. I use this feature and find it valuable for connecting with executives and otherwise hard-to-reach prospects.

How to Import Contacts to LinkedIn

LinkedIn makes it really easy to import contacts from your mail system, and does NOT send annoying automatic emails to your contacts. Instead, LinkedIn will display your list of your contacts, including details about who is already using LinkedIn and how many contacts they have, and then you can manually check the boxes for the people you want to send connection invitations to.

To import your contacts, visit your LinkedIn profile and click on "Add Connections" in the upper right corner. Follow the steps to import contacts from whatever email system you use.

Note that if you use Microsoft Outlook like I do, you will need to export your contacts to a CSV file that can then be imported to LinkedIn.

How to Export Contacts from Outlook:

Click on File > Import and Export
Choose Export to a File and click Next
Choose Comma Separated Values (DOS) and click Next
Select the contact folder you want to export and click Next
In the Save File As field, decide where you want to save the file (I usually save mine to my Desktop) and give the file a name like "Contacts."

Click Next, and then click Finish. Your file will be generated and you can then import it to LinkedIn.

LinkedIn Groups

LinkedIn Groups are remarkably active, covering a wide variety of mostly business-related topics. Once again, here you can search for groups by keyword such as city name or industry. Look for groups that reach your target audience and get involved. Answer questions, ask questions, and be engaging. It's also quite easy to start your own group on LinkedIn, which can be a great way to gain visibility in your industry.

I run the Nonfiction Authors Network on LinkedIn, which grew to 1,000+ members in a matter of months. This has been a fabulous way to attract my target audience for publishing services while allowing me to demonstrate my authority in the related subject matter.

When you join groups on LinkedIn, check the setting to receive a daily digest of message board discussions via email. This allows you to quickly scan conversations to see if there is anything interesting that you want to comment on. When you post a comment on a group message board, all members can view your comment and may also choose to view your profile.

Also, on the sidebar for each group is a list of "Most Influential Contributors" to the group. When you engage on a regular basis, you can get featured there, bringing even more exposure.

LinkedIn Engagement Tips

❖ Fill out your profile as completely as possible. Be descriptive, include work history, and fill out as many fields as possible. Keywords are powerful on LinkedIn and a complete profile will help you get found by the right people.

❖ Take advantage of applications on LinkedIn such as BlogLink, which will import your blog feed directly onto your profile. Click on the "Add an Application" link on your profile page to find lots of options.

❖ If you want to reach contacts at major companies, invest in a paid LinkedIn account, which is an inexpensive way to receive InMail credits, plus the ability to track who has viewed your profile.

❖ Share new blog posts and other useful content on LinkedIn, just as you do on Facebook and Twitter.

❖ Ask past clients to write recommendations for you. These can be influential in helping you land additional business opportunities.

❖ The big action on LinkedIn happens in the groups. Join at least two or three groups where your niche audience spends time.

❖ Better yet, start a group on LinkedIn. Find a unique approach to your topic and invite people to participate.

Google Plus

In 2011, Google launched Google Plus (http://plus.google.com), a social network that clearly wants to go head-to-head with Facebook and Twitter. To use this service, you must start with a free Google account, and then you can populate your Plus profile and begin building your network.

At the heart of this service are circles, which come with some pre-defined categories: friends, family, and acquaintances. You can drag and drop Google Plus users into any of these circles, or those that you define yourself (such as business contacts, leads, etc.). With circles, you can share content specifically with a chosen circle or view content from those in a specific circle. Similar to following someone on Twitter, just because you add someone to one of your circles does not mean that person will do the same for you.

Of course, this service has many social media standards: the ability to chat with users, share photos, play games, and send invitations. There's also a somewhat sales-y pitch to incorporate your Google Plus account with Gmail.

One unique feature that Google Plus offers is called "Sparks." When you tell Google what your topics of interest are, Google will provide recommended content for you to view from around the web. You can also create a "Hangout" and conduct a video-based chat with up to 10 users.

Prior to Google Plus, Google introduced its "+1" button, which you'll notice hovering next to links on search results. When you click on the +1 button for a link to an article, blog post, or business that you like, you give that link some added social currency. Your chosen +1 selections also appear on your Google Plus profile.

There is still much debate about how Google Plus and the +1 feature will affect SEO for websites and pages, though one has to speculate that the social currency created here will be factored into the equation. There is also the big question of whether users will embrace Google Plus when Facebook, Twitter, and LinkedIn all have a firm hold on users.

This is also not Google's first trip to the rodeo. It hasn't had much success with previous social media services—Orkut, Google Wave, and Google Buzz all failed to build an audience. At the time of this writing, the role of Google Plus in social media and internet visibility remains to be seen. However, I will add that there is evidence that sharing via Google Plus, particularly with the +1 feature, can give your posts a boost when it comes to SEO.

Social Media Time Management

By far, one of the biggest concerns about using social media is the amount of time it takes to manage. It does take some time to get started, get your profiles set up, and begin building a following. But it doesn't have to be a full-time job. Studies have shown that most marketers using social media spend less than an hour per day managing their networks.

Sample Social Media Activity

Here is what your week might look like when managing your social media presence.

Monday

(The busiest day of the week due to weekend catch-up and scheduling for the week)

8:15 a.m.: Log in to HootSuite and share your most recent blog post with Facebook, LinkedIn, and Twitter. Next, hop on over to Facebook to check your fan page for any new messages.

8:20 a.m.: Log in to LinkedIn to view and accept connection requests and check inbox for messages.

8:25 a.m.: Check out Twitter activity on TweetDeck. Reply to any messages sent to you or find an interesting post from someone else to retweet.

11:20 a.m.: Since you have a few minutes between appointments, check TweetDeck to view messages and respond. Always look for something interesting to retweet, or send out an interesting post with some other news from your day. If you have time, take a quick look at Facebook to see what's happening there.

1:15 p.m.: In between projects, take a quick look at TweetDeck and find something interesting to share.

3:40 p.m.: With a few minutes to spare between appointments, repeat steps from above. Check TweetDeck and Facebook for updates and find a reason to engage. Or, if you have something new to share, log in to HootSuite and send an update out to all of your networks.

5:00 p.m.: Take one last look at TweetDeck before you end your workday.

Total Time Spent: 40 minutes

Tuesday

8:00 a.m.: Take a few minutes to check out the activity in your groups. Respond to a couple of questions, ask a question, or share a link to some industry news. Check TweetDeck and Facebook for morning activity.

9:50 a.m.: You have a few minutes to spare, so check TweetDeck for updates and reply as needed. If you come across an interesting post, retweet it to your network.

1:15 p.m.: You've added a new blog post. Log in to HootSuite and share the title and a link (shortened with bit.ly) with your networks. Also schedule it to re-publish on Twitter several times over the coming weeks.

3:50 p.m.: Check out TweetDeck and Facebook for comments and activity from your blog post link. Reply or send a thanks to those who shared the information via retweet or commented on your post.

5:00 p.m.: No time left in the day, so you skip it and wait until tomorrow.

Total Time Spent: 30 minutes

Does that all sound doable? Repeat as needed during the week and soon, social media will become part of your daily routine. And when you start seeing results, it might even become a part of your day that you enjoy!

Social Media Success Roundup

❖ Engage with your audience. While you can automate some of your social media activity, remember to show that there is a human being behind your profile.

❖ Participate often. Some amount of activity on a daily basis is best for maximum exposure. Remember that not everyone views their networks at the same time. For best visibility, rotate activity among your networks throughout the day.

❖ Balance your content and sales activity. Most businesses (with the exception of retail) should follow the 90/10 rule: 90% useful content, 10% sales.

❖ Be unique. Figure out how to set your business apart from your competitors. You can do this by being a resource for your community, sharing interesting content, holding contests, co-promoting with other businesses, and ultimately, building loyalty.

❖ Have a goal for your brand. What do you want to be known for? Who do you want to connect with? Be clear with your messaging.

❖ Add your Twitter, Facebook, and LinkedIn profile links to your website and blog for maximum visibility. Links should be embedded in corresponding logos and featured in prime real estate on your website (like on the header for your site or on top of the sidebar across your entire site).

❖ Promote your profile links in your email signature, in your electronic newsletter, online profiles, and anywhere you have online visibility.

❖ Connect with the people you want following you. In other words, seek out your target audience. Follow them on Twitter and locate groups on LinkedIn where they congregate. Spend at least an hour each week building your network.

❖ Pay attention to how others are using social media. This is an evolving medium. Look for what you like and don't like about how others are using their networks. Always be on the lookout for ways to grow and stand out. Most importantly, <u>do what feels right to you</u>! There are a lot of people giving advice on this subject. You can learn from plenty of sources, and each will likely offer different advice, so pick and choose which advice makes sense to you.

Develop Your Social Media Strategy

❖ What do you want to be known for online?

❖ What ideas can you come up with that are outside of the box?

❖ How can you provide content that attracts your niche audience?

❖ How can you get their attention?

❖ Where will your content come from and how often?

❖ What can you do that is fun, funny, interesting, or noteworthy?

❖ How can you build buzz for your services?

❖ Who can you collaborate with?

❖ What contests could you hold to generate activity?

❖ What kinds of groups would be valuable for you?

Entrepreneur Interview
Name: Neal Schaffer

Business name: Windmills Marketing
Website URL: http://windmillnetworking.com
Social media links:

> http://www.linkedin.com/in/nealschaffer
> http://www.twitter.com/nealschaffer
> http://www.facebook.com/windmillnetworking
> http://www.gplus.to/nealschaffer
> http://www.youtube.com/user/windmillnetworking1
> http://www.stumbleupon.com/stumbler/nealschaffer

Tell us about your business and what you do:

I work as an executive in charge of social media strategy for two different social media agencies: Social 5150 (which targets English-speaking markets) as well as Green Dream Social (which targets Spanish-speaking audiences). I also directly help smaller businesses on their social media strategy, while helping professionals and company employees leverage social media as a business tool under the Windmill Networking brand through social media coaching, public speaking, and writing books. I am the author of *Maximizing LinkedIn for Sales and Social Media Marketing* and *Windmill Networking: Understanding, Leveraging and Maximizing LinkedIn.*

Who is your target audience?

My target audience are those businesses and professionals learning to leverage social media as a business tool at every stage of development: from beginning their first foray into social media, to understanding how to get to the next level in their social media efforts, and finally, to maximizing the ROI from their frequent use of social media in their business. As an executive in two different social media agencies, I now have the infrastructure and backbone to take on large clients who increasingly need more help with their social business efforts.

How did you get started in your business?

My business actually started organically. After I wrote my first book, *Windmill Networking: Understanding, Leveraging and Maximizing LinkedIn*, I was invited to speak at a number of business and social media conferences. Soon thereafter, I was simultaneously approached by multiple local businesses looking for help with their social media efforts. I decided at that time that businesses needed both education as well as a strategic approach, and I soon thereafter formed my social media consulting practice, Windmills Marketing. Recently, businesses need more help in implementing their social media strategy, as well as adding human resources who have a deep expertise in social media, so in order to take on these larger clients, I folded my social media consulting business into these two agencies.

What are some of the best tactics you have used to build your audience and establish your authority online?

Social media is all about communication and information. The best tactics I have used have been in creating content to display my expertise, as well as engaging with those who might be interested in my services in various social media communities. Through continuing to do this, and sharing information of others that my relevant audience might be interested in when I had none of my own information to share, I have slowly become the "channel" for many to tune in to when they want to learn more about social media. It takes time, and sticking to a routine, but I believe any business in any niche can have results within three to six months if they follow this example.

How has social media impacted your business? Any success stories you can share?

Seeing that my business itself is selling social media services, my marketing has been done predominantly using social media. Without social media, my business could not have existed. Furthermore, all of my business comes from either word-of-mouth referrals or social media. My favorite social media success story is from a competitor's LinkedIn Group. I subscribed to a weekly digest of activity and noticed one discussion had generated a few hundred comments. I navigated to the most recent comment and felt like replying to the question that the LinkedIn user had posed. Instead of commenting in the discussion, I viewed the profile of the user and realized that we lived in the same county. I contacted him, offering to meet over a cup of coffee to answer his questions about social media. When we met, he confided in me that his client was looking for someone with social media expertise, and one week later I was introduced to his client and signed a consulting deal.

Do you engage in any communities and if so, how has that impacted your business?

Business has always been social, and thus networking, both online and offline, is an essential aspect to building out any business. When building out my own business, I both created in-person networking groups as well as online communities in social media websites. I also regularly attended local business networking meetings. These days, I spend more time interacting on the largest internet forum of all, Twitter, but I still try to go out and meet people at networking events to continually nurture my network – and develop new business. As my social media success story indicated, I have also developed business as well as created relationships of value through LinkedIn Groups participation.

What role does content play in your marketing strategy?

As someone who is trying to sell services to other businesses, content is the essential tool that can be used to engage with others online, show your expertise, and build up authority for your brand. My primary content focus is blogging, and I consider a blog post playing the same role as an advertisement for my company. My books are also great marketing pieces in themselves. The other important aspect about content, in a social media marketing context, is to also share the content of others, which indirectly helps build up your subject-matter authority in social media communities.

What advice would you offer to readers who want to promote their business online?

Your online marketing efforts should obviously begin with, and be governed by, a strategy. A mistake that many businesses do is to just jump in without a plan and run blindly with their marketing activities. You can waste a lot of time and money in doing so. A strategy will help you better understand your own objectives as well as the specific steps that you can take to use online marketing to help you achieve success. If you are not confident in your understanding, hire a consultant to help educate and guide you in creating your strategy. Once you start implementing online marketing governed by your strategy, you can begin to monitor what is effective and what isn't working, making tweaks to your tactics and maximizing your return on investment. Of course, your strategy should be a living document and maintained as the online landscape changes over time.

If you were starting your business over today, is there anything you would do differently?

As someone who is providing a service, the challenge is always in differentiating your service from others. That is why I have always wanted to create a product of my own that would be separate from my service, and although I have had various product ideas, I have yet to pull the trigger on this. I am finally starting to execute on this, but it is something I should have done earlier on when there was a greater window of opportunity for it.

Is there anything else you would like to add?

Social media is the ultimate game-changer—similar to how the internet was two decades ago—that can help establish a new brand or help your company more deeply engage with present customers and potential clients. Recent reports said that the average spent on social media by businesses is 10% of their marketing budget, but that number is going up. I would approach social media aggressively and understand how to naturally integrate it into everything that your company does, using 10% as a guide as to what is the minimum you should be investing in your social efforts.

Chapter Eight
Content Marketing Tactics

"The critical ingredient is getting off your butt and doing something. It's as simple as that. A lot of people have ideas, but there are few who decide to do something about them now. Not tomorrow. Not next week. But today. The true entrepreneur is a doer, not a dreamer."
—Nolan Bushnell (Creator of Atari game systems and Chuck E. Cheese's Pizza-Time Theater)

When you think about marketing your business online, it can seem overwhelming. There are so many sites and strategies and techniques to learn, and of course, for a busy entrepreneur there is never enough time in a day.

This chapter covers a multitude of ways to further promote your services online using the power of content, but I want to be very clear: *You don't have to do all of them.* In fact, I don't know anyone who does all of the things listed here, myself included. Instead, read through these options and then consider which ones best fit your business. Roll out any new strategies one at a time so that you avoid getting overwhelmed and maximize your ability to track results.

Social Bookmarking

Social bookmarking sites like StumbleUpon, Digg, Delicious, and Reddit provide a way to create public online bookmarks for content. Each of these sites works a little differently, but the bottom line is the same: the goal is to get people to bookmark your content so that it gets greater visibility.

For example, when a user gives a "Digg" to an article or blog post, it counts toward the popularity of that piece. As more Diggs are given by readers, the article works its way up the popularity list with the ultimate goal being home page placement—which brings plenty of eyeballs.

It's not easy to achieve priority placement on these sites since your content must be quite popular to do so. Also, a very small percentage of internet users actually take the time to give social bookmarking currency, so if you have 1,000 readers for a blog post, you'll be lucky if 1% to 5% make the effort. However, those who do achieve top placement on Digg and the other sites report great rewards from added traffic and overall visibility.

If you want to encourage your readers to bookmark your content, make it easy for them by installing bookmarking buttons on your blog. Blog platforms such as WordPress and TypePad offer simple plug-ins to make this easy. Also, you should become a registered user of these sites yourself. If you want others to choose your content, you need to reciprocate and participate by choosing their content, too.

Promote with Video

Videos can be a great option for businesses that have a visual component. You can create and promote videos to showcase your services, feature client testimonials, demonstrate how to do something, tour your facilities, teach a lesson, conduct an interview, or provide entertainment. For creative minds, the options are endless.

While videos should be showcased on your website, they should also be added to video sharing sites like YouTube, Vimeo, Viddler, and Ustream. Free video sharing sites bring viewers to your content, and ultimately, traffic back to your website because these sites get priority placement in Google.

I just conducted a Google search on "how to bake a chocolate pie." Sure enough, a video tagged on YouTube with that exact search phrase appears in the top five search results. When searching for "how to tie a tie," a YouTube video appears in the top three results. You will find similar results for just about any "how-to" phrase you type into Google. Why not get in on that action?

The most popular clips on YouTube are instructional, funny, inspirational, or controversial. In most cases, shorter videos of five minutes or less are also better than longer videos. YouTube visitors rate videos and the more views a video receives, the higher up it moves in the ranks.

You can get the momentum started by promoting your videos to your customers and via your social media outlets. Be sure to include your company information or website URL either at the bottom of the video or in the last frame of the video, and properly tag your video's page with a keyword-rich title and description.

Incidentally, one of the great benefits of video is that it doesn't have to be an expensive undertaking. A simple flip video camera (retails for around $100) can do the job, and files can be easily imported online.

Podcasts and Audio Recordings

Have you noticed that more and more websites have audio built right into the pages? Some start talking as you land on the page (something I don't recommend), while others offer a control box where you can decide if you want to hear the recorded message.

Keep in mind that we all learn differently. Some learn better visually and others learn by listening. When you add audio recordings to a website you reach auditory learners. You can use audio clips to introduce your company, describe a special offer, or explain the features of a product or service. New technology makes it easy to create recordings and embed them right into your website.

You can run an internet search for "audio recording software" and find dozens of choices, or pick up some equipment from your local electronics store. I have personally used Audio Acrobat (www. audioacrobat.com). This is a handy service that allows you to create recordings using your phone and save them in MP3 format. It's quick and easy to use, and the price is reasonable.

Podcasts are usually defined as a series of online recordings (though you can call a single recording a podcast and nobody will argue). Users can download podcasts to listen on their computers, iPods, iPads, or iPhones.

When used for marketing purposes, podcasts are usually comprised of instructional programs or interviews. You can make them available from your website, though you can also import them to iTunes. For the latest instructions on how to do this, see http://www.apple.com/itunes/podcasts/specs.html.

Note that hosting a podcast series can be a great way to attract new prospects and keep your audience engaged on a consistent basis. Search some of the podcasts on iTunes to get ideas about how others use this popular technology.

Teleseminars and Webinars

A teleseminar is essentially a conference call held over the phone to a broad audience, while a webinar adds a visual component on the computer—usually a presentation or online demonstration of some sort. I am a fan of both options, provided they're conducted without too much hype.

Teleseminars can be a great outlet for attracting an audience and introducing people to your services. For example, a real estate agent could conduct a teleseminar on how to become a first-time home buyer. Offer this as a free event and require registration to participate, and you can capture contact information from interested participants while providing informative content—all while demonstrating your authority in your field.

A common format for teleseminars is to conduct an interview of another expert in a subject of interest to your target audience. This format has grown a little tired from overuse so if you do it, make sure yours has a unique focus and interesting guests and topics. Allow time for Q&A at the end to give your audience added value for participating.

Unfortunately, teleseminars have been overused and abused online. Some marketers use them as part of their churn-and-burn strategy, offering free teleseminars with big breakthrough promises, only to avoid giving any actual real value, and then ending with a big, fat, hairy sales pitch.

I like to give people the benefit of the doubt and I love to learn something new, so over the years I've participated in plenty of these events, only to end up disappointed and losing all respect for the host when expectations weren't met or an over-the-top sales pitch was given. Don't let this happen to you! If you make a promise online, keep it—and always provide value, even if you're asking for a sale at the end. It is perfectly acceptable to ask for a sale, and I would argue that if you actually made every minute of that call count with great information, you'd end up with more sales as a result.

Webinars can be conducted in much the same way as teleseminars. They can be quite useful for events that require a visual presentation or demonstration. One company that leverages webinars as a promotion tool is Office Depot. Their Web Café series features popular authors, speakers, and other authorities who deliver content-rich presentations. I was invited to give a presentation for this series and was impressed to learn that these sessions regularly generate thousands of sign-ups. As a featured speaker, I also heard from participants for months after my presentation, since many found the archived recording later on.

This brings up another point: You don't have to be the host. As an authority in your field, there are many advantages to serving as a guest on other people's teleseminars and webinars. If they already have an audience established, you can gain valuable added exposure with that audience, with very little effort on your part other than to deliver great content.

Teleseminar and Webinar Service Providers

❖ http://instantteleseminar.com

❖ http://freeconference.com

❖ http://gotomeeting.com

❖ http://webex.com

❖ http://intercall.com

How to Host Your Own Teleseminar

1. Decide on a topic and how you plan to deliver it. Will it be a Q&A with a guest, will someone interview you, or will you be the sole speaker leading a lecture? Can you do something really unique and hold an open Q&A with the audience for an hour? Get creative!

2. Write a compelling title and description of the event.

3. Sign up for a service such as www.freeconference.com or www.instantteleseminar.com. Both offer recording features, though

you may want to add a backup recording option via www.
audioacrobat.com.

4. You will need a way to manage registrations, either with an
online shopping cart or another service. One option is to create
an account with www.eventbrite.com, which helps with managing registration. There is no charge to manage free events and
they charge a small transaction fee for paid events.

5. Promote your event in as many places as possible. Here are
some to include:

   ❖ Create an event on Facebook and LinkedIn

   ❖ Announce your event via all of your social media networks
   and repeat several times before the event takes place

   ❖ Post to www.craigslist.org for several cities

   ❖ Post to sites such as www.selfgrowth.com, www.semina-
   rannouncer.com, and www.events.org

   ❖ Also post to any other sites where your target audience
   is located. This can include newsletters, message boards,
   classifieds, forums, online groups, and any place that can
   bring exposure for the appropriate audience.

6. Be sure to create a script for your event so that you have a
strong opening and closing message and enough content in
between. Consider how you want to address the audience.
Allowing questions at any time can disrupt the flow of the call.
I recommend muting the line during the presentation and then
opening up the line for questions a couple of times during the
call or once at the end.

Article Marketing

For years I have marketed my business with articles. This is accomplished by writing an interesting how-to piece and making it available
to other websites, blogs, and e-newsletters along with a brief author bio.

Even though you should not directly promote your business in
an article, readers will visit your site if they like what you have to say.
Publishing articles also builds your credibility in your field, expands

your exposure to a broad audience, and adds links back to your website, which helps with search engine optimization.

Many websites operate on a limited budget and appreciate articles written by experts. You can offer to swap articles with website owners and co-promote each other, or simply submit your article for consideration. Most sites that accept articles will feature "Submission Guidelines" somewhere within the site. If you can't locate guidelines, contact the site owner or editor and ask if he or she is interested in reviewing your article for possible inclusion.

The best way to decide who you want to write for is to look for websites that reach your target audience. Check out trade associations as these often have newsletters or articles online. You can also search the internet for industry keywords and begin building a list of sites where you can potentially be published.

Also look for opportunities to distribute your articles locally. Your local newspapers and magazines might be thrilled to feature you in a column either online or in print.

There are also numerous content sites that allow you to post articles that others can reprint on their websites and in their newsletters. This is a great opportunity to showcase your business. Following are some of my favorite article content sites:

- ❖ www.ideamarketers.com
- ❖ www.ezinearticles.com
- ❖ www.goarticles.com
- ❖ www.scribd.com
- ❖ www.articlesbase.com

A word of caution about article marketing: Ideally, you should limit the number of times the same article appears online. If it's picked up by multiple websites, Google will not display all instances of the article. For best results, modify parts of the article and title when distributing to various websites. Regardless, you will still gain great exposure by distributing content when it is picked up across many sites.

Writing Your Articles

You don't have to spend a lot of time or effort on writing articles—really! In fact, some of the best articles are the ones that are brief and to the point. Remember that you are writing these for publication online, so articles that are short and sweet are appreciated. Sub-headings and bullets are also recommended because they make it much easier to read on a computer screen.

How-to articles are the most popular variety. Keep the process simple by using top-10-style lists. For example, "Seven Ways to Get Kids Ready for Back-to-School" or "13 Steps to Beautiful Skin." Titles are also important because they are what initially grab a reader's interest. Try to make yours as appealing as possible.

Repurpose, Reuse, Recycle

Make sure you reuse the articles that you submit to websites for publication. You can also submit articles to print publications. The major magazines at the checkout stands are difficult to break into and won't accept reprints; however, there are dozens of smaller publications, trade association newsletters, and small city newspapers that will gladly accept well-written articles.

Visit your local bookstore to find a variety of smaller magazines. You can also search Google to find industry publications.

Here is an example of how to format an email submission for an article:

Subject: Article Submission — 10 Super-Foods for Better Hair and Skin

By Susan Smith

<Insert Article Text>

About the Author:

Susan Smith is a nutritionist specializing in women's health issues. For more information, visit <website.com>.

*You are welcome to reprint this article provided the author bio is included. Thank you very much for your consideration.

Note that nine times out of ten you won't receive a response from editors—they are simply too busy. More often than not, you won't even know that your article ran until you see it yourself, it shows up in your Google Alerts, or you hear about it from a reader. Who cares if you hear about it; the point is that it was printed!

Information Products

Information products include books, ebooks, reports, white papers, videos, audio recordings, workbooks, worksheets, databases, booklets, and any other way that you can compile and deliver information. While you can sell these products for profit—and we will cover this topic in the Internet Revenue Streams chapter—you can also give away information for marketing purposes.

For service providers, one of the most obvious places to give away information is with your newsletter subscribers. To add incentive for signing up, provide something of value such as a report, recording, or ebook. For example, an estate attorney might offer a report called 15 Ways to Protect Your Family and Your Assets. A ghostwriter might offer an ebook covering Book Marketing Strategies You Need to Tackle Before You Write the Book.

Information can be given away for all kinds of situations. If you host a booth at a trade show, offer a free ebook to anyone who stops by to chat. If you conduct speaking engagements, give away a booklet of tips—something that attendees will want to keep after the fact. A life coach could offer a downloadable workbook from her website. An insurance agent could distribute a disaster-planning guide to alliance partners that can be co-branded and given to prospects.

I stopped using boring sales brochures years ago and instead give away all kinds of information. My reports, ebooks, and recordings have been given away through my own site, as a bonus with new product and service offerings, at speaking engagements, and by alliance partners for distribution with their audiences.

Presentations

If you create PowerPoint presentations, check out www.slideshare.com. You can post your presentations here for others to view. Also, if you give a presentation and want to make your slides available to attendees, this is a great spot to post them. Even better, LinkedIn offers a SlideShare application so that you can post your presentations to your LinkedIn profile (look for the "Add Application" link from your profile page). If you share a link to a SlideShare presentation on Facebook, users will be able to view your presentation directly on your Facebook page. I love technology!

Tracking Content with Google Alerts

Google offers a lot of useful services and one of my favorites is Google Alerts: http://alerts.google.com. This free tool allows you to designate keywords and get notified via email when they are mentioned on websites, blogs, online news channels, and more.

Here are ways to leverage Google Alerts for your business:

1. **Business Name** – Keep track of websites that mention your company. This is an opportunity to send a note of thanks or address an issue if something derogatory is posted, like a complaint about customer service. Big companies track mentions of their businesses online and you should, too.

2. **Personal Name** – Find out where you're mentioned online. This is especially important for authors, speakers, celebrities, and individual service providers.

3. **Website** – Track where your website is mentioned by creating an alert for your domain. Leave off the leading "www" and instead just specify your domain and extension, such as "authoritypublishing.com."

4. **Blog** – If you host a blog, follow the website guidelines above to create an alert for your blog domain.

5. **Titles** – If you distribute articles for online marketing purposes, create an alert for each article title so that you can track where your articles appear. Authors can use this same strategy for tracking mentions of your book titles.

6. **Industry Research** – To stay on top of industry news, create alerts for keywords and key phrases for your industry.

For example, I have an alert for "publishing industry." This makes it easy to stay on top of news, competition, trends, and much more.

7. **Competitive Research** – If you want to find out who is talking about your competition or where they are being mentioned, create alerts for each competitor's business name and/or website URL.

8. **Lead Generation** – If breaking news can produce leads for your company, use Google Alerts for related phrases. For example, if you own a human resources firm and want to find out what companies are hiring in Sacramento, you could create several alerts: "now hiring Sacramento," "job posting Sacramento," and "job listing Sacramento."

9. **Lead Research** – If there is a company or client that you want to land, create alerts to stay on top of their most recent online activity. This can provide valuable insight into what the company is up to and who is talking about them.

10. **Client Research** – Track activity for your top 10 or 20 existing clients. This can give you valuable insight into what they're up to, and also provide you with reasons to contact them. For example, if one of your clients receives major media coverage, you will learn about it right away and can send them a note of congratulations.

Google Search Tips

Exact Keyword Search: You can specify exact keywords by putting a plus sign (+) in front of the word. For example, if you search for the word "publish," Google search results would include "publishing" and "publisher." Adding a plus sign to the beginning of the word (+publish) will ensure that you only receive exact matches.

Exact Key Phrase Search: When you search for a phrase, Google results will return anything that includes all of the words in the phrase—not that exact phrase. But if you enclose your search in quotes ("how to publish a book"), the results will only include that exact phrase.

Alternate Keyword: To return a search with alternate results, use "OR" between the words (the letters "O" and "R" must be capitalized). For example, "author OR writer" will return results with either keyword. For a more complex search, you can put part of the phrase in parentheses: (author OR writer) "business books."

Synonyms: If you want your search results to return related terms, use a tilde (~) in front of the word. For example, if you use this feature to search for the word "~author," Google returns results that include "book," "writer," and "literature."

Search a Single Website: If you want to track new entries on a specific site, you can use the "site:" operator. For example, if you want to track mentions of business books on the *New York Times* website, your search would look like this: "business book" site:nytimes.com.

Entrepreneur Interview
Name: Denise O'Berry

Business name: The Small Business Edge Corp
Website URL: http://www.deniseoberry.com
Social media links:

> http://www.twitter.com/deniseoberry
> http://www.facebook.com/smallbusinesscashflow
> http://www.youtube.com/deniseoberry
> http://www.deniseoberry.com/+

Tell us about your business and what you do:

My focus is on providing tips, tools, and advice to help small-business owners be successful. Most small-business owners and solopreneurs spend lots of time hunting for the next great thing that will make running their business easier and help improve their bottom line. They want a business that helps them make the most of the lifestyle they have dreamed of—not necessarily some glitzy life lounging on the beach sipping mai tais—but a life that fits for them. I aim to help them do that through my website.

There are lots of tips and tools on the site that will help them do just that.

- Marketing tips that will help get the word out to prospects and clients
- Ways to improve cash flow and pump up that bottom line
- Resources and tools that can help make business life a whole lot easier and less hectic

No matter what the obstacles are, small-business people are a very hardy lot. Their enthusiasm and ability to overcome huge obstacles inspires me to provide the best tools and tips I can to help them be successful.

Who is your target audience?

My target is what I call micro businesses. That's a business with 0 to 10 employees. Most of the people I serve are solopreneurs with no employees. It's really tough for those folks because they have so many hats to wear on any given day. So I work to provide the resources that will make it easier for them.

How did you get started in your business?

I've worked with hundreds of small-business owners over the years. I began my consulting firm in 1996 because I saw small businesses struggling everywhere I looked. We wear so many hats, and sometimes it just takes a little help from an "outsider" to kick us in the right direction.

At that time, I was consulting one-on-one with small-business owners who were looking to improve their business. It was quite a thrill to help a struggling business owner move to success. I don't provide face-to-face service anymore, but do help that same audience through the tools I have created and the tips I provide on my website and through my "Small Biz Tips Weekly" newsletter.

What are some of the best tactics you have used to build your audience and establish your authority online?

The best thing I've done is worked to build relationships with other small-business owners around the world. The internet makes that easy to do. But you have to do two things: 1) show up, and 2) participate. I have made so many connections with people since I began online in 1998—many of whom I've yet to meet in person. Through these connections, I've been able to reach thousands of small-business owners who may never have heard of me otherwise.

How has social media impacted your business? Any success stories you can share?

Social media is one of the best tools a small-business owner can use. The internet helps break down the entry barrier for small business, and social media makes it possible for small-business owners to reach their market anywhere in the world.

I've been participating in the social aspect of the internet since I came online in 1998. Back then, there was no social media. Social networking isn't a new phenomenon. It's driven by a natural human tendency to connect with others. At the time, we called it "networking on the internet." I was so sold on the benefits of this new type of networking that I started speaking at local functions and ended up being invited to speak at a national NAWBO conference, which really helped spread the word. News of my efforts got picked up by a regional TV station, and I was one of their featured stories in 2000. You can see that here: http://www.deniseoberry.com/bn9.

In 2003, I started a community forum of small-business owners online called Minding Your Own Business (MYOB). It was an awesome community of small-business owners who helped each other and shared tips and resources so everyone could be successful. I closed the forum and moved on to other things in 2008 after growing it to more than 2,300 members. The network is now closed, but is still archived online—nothing ever dies on the internet. There is tons of good information there for small business. You can find it at http://www.deniseoberry.com/myob.

Today's social media technology allows us to connect faster and easier than ever before. It has allowed me to stretch my reach even farther to every corner of the earth so I can build relationships with other small-business owners, discover their needs, and provide the tools necessary to help them out.

Do you engage in any communities and if so, how has that impacted your business?

There are so many online communities where we can connect with others. The key is to find one or two that work for your business. We can only stretch our time so far, and any more than that is just too tough.

One of my favorite groups is a mastermind group of small-business owners online. It is so helpful to be part of a trusting group of people who will provide you feedback and advice when you need it. Otherwise, it can get pretty lonely trying to run a small business.

My favorite group is Solo Masterminds, led by Kelly McCausey. I met Kelly in the early 2000s in an online forum and didn't meet her in person until 2009. With Solo Masterminds, she has built an awesome membership community of small-business owners. You can find the info here: http://www.deniseoberry.com/go/solo.

Although I no longer participate directly in offline groups, they are incredibly valuable in making connections with others who are on the same path. The first few years of my business, I was very active in two key associations that helped my business grow.

What role does content play in your marketing strategy?

All types of content play a big role in my marketing strategy. I started my first blog in 2004. Because of that blog, I was invited to write at allbusiness.com, a huge small-business portal. While writing there, I was discovered by my editor from Wiley and invited to write my book, *Small Business Cash Flow: Strategies for Making Your Business a Financial Success.*

I make sure my content is repurposed across as many platforms as possible. That means a blog post can turn into a white paper, which can turn into a video and a podcast. A collection of blog posts can easily be turned into an ebook (free or paid). Content that is only used once is wasted. It's important to leverage as much of your content as you can to extend your reach.

What advice would you offer to readers who want to promote their business online?

The primary key to your success is to DO something. Way too many small-business owners spend time buying tools and learning, then never put it into action. You must DO.

Take some time to identify where your market hangs out online and leverage that to your advantage. Don't just promote somewhere because it worked for someone else. Determine whether it might work for you before you leap and if it will, DO it.

If you were starting your business over today, is there anything you would do differently?

Yes, be stingy with cash. A business can't survive without cash flow. Every decision about every expenditure should be scrutinized to determine if the money really needs to be spent. In the early days of a business, small-business owners need to have a buffer of cash to rely on while they get their marketing machine going. That takes time.

Quick Tip

Make sure you list **http://** *in front of your website URL anytime you post it online. For example:*

Don't type it like this:
www.BusinessInfoGuide.com

Instead, type this:
http://BusinessInfoGuide.com

While some email providers and website pages will automatically activate a website link, many will leave the link static. This means that users will have to copy and paste the link in a browser to view the site. Using http:// activates your link to make it clickable from most email systems and web pages.

Chapter Nine

Hype-Free Internet Marketing

"The wisest men follow their own direction."
—Euripides

So far, you've learned to establish your authority in your field, drive more website traffic, convert site visitors into buyers, leverage social media, and promote content. But wait, there's more! Once again, you don't need to use all of these strategies. Choose the ones that work best for you.

Internet Radio

One promotion opportunity that I believe is under-utilized is internet radio. These programs often focus on a niche topic such as selling on eBay or parenting for busy moms. Though few reach hundreds of thousands of listeners like traditional talk radio, many reach 1,000 or more listeners who are specifically interested in the topic at hand. Even better, guests are often featured for fifteen minutes up to a full hour. Guests are also promoted online before and after the interview since most archive recordings online. Best of all, you can conduct interviews from anywhere. All you need is a reliable land line to dial in.

As an authority in your field, you can be a great guest for internet radio shows. I have conducted countless internet radio interviews over the years to promote my books and my business. Most shows are hosted weekly—some daily. All need guests and make it easy to contact them with your pitch.

When pitching shows, you want to recommend a topic of interest to the show's target audience. Ideally, your topic should teach them how to do something and should never be blatantly self-promotional. This is another area where you have the chance to demonstrate your authority in your field, and by providing great information the audience will naturally want to learn more about you. Another way to make these shows pay off is to offer a free information product to the audience as a download in exchange for signing up for your mailing list.

When it comes to conducting radio interviews, I like to provide show producers with my media sheet, which includes sample interview questions as well as short and long versions of my bio. This helps the host prepare for the interview, and makes sure he or she has the most up-to-date information available.

Not every host will use your proposed interview questions, though in my experience, most are grateful to receive this information. Simply send it along once you've booked an engagement and be prepared for anything. The host may ask you a few questions from your list or none at all. Radio guests should be prepared to take curve balls!

Your media sheet doesn't need to be fancy, though including some graphic elements will help it stand out. I use a simple header with my photo, book covers, and website URL's. The document is created and maintained in Word, though I save it as a PDF before sending it along. As a general rule, PDF documents look more professional and can also be read across all kinds of platforms, including PC, Mac, and mobile phones.

By the way, you may want to consider starting your own internet radio show. The vast majority of show hosts are authorities in their fields and use their shows as a platform for attracting clients and getting more exposure online.

To find shows that reach your target audience, search sites including http://blogtalkradio.com, http://alltalkradio.com, http://wsradio.com, and http://womensradio.com. I also sell lists of internet radio shows and podcasts, which you can find in the Store section of either http://authoritypublishing.com or http://businessinfoguide.com. There you can also download my free report called, "How to Pitch Yourself as a Guest for Radio Interviews."

Here's a sample radio pitch:

Proposed Topic: How to market your business by writing and publishing books and ebooks.

Did you know that a recent survey showed that more than 80% of Americans would like to write a book? At the same time, businesses are looking for new marketing strategies and ways to stay competitive in a challenging economy. Promoting a business with a book can be a powerful way to gain a competitive advantage, and it's easier to accomplish than you might think.

As a guest on your show, I would propose discussing the following key points:

- How businesses can use books for marketing purposes

- Simple strategies for writing a book quickly

- Publishing options, including traditional and self-publishing

- Options with ebooks for the Kindle, iPhone, iPad, Nook, and more

- Methods for building buzz online

I have years of experience as a radio show guest and I can assure you that our time together will be well-spent and focused on delivering value to your audience. I would also be happy to provide you with sample interview questions and a complimentary copy of my book at your request.

Thank you very much for your consideration. I look forward to hearing back from you soon.

Warm regards,

Stephanie Chandler

<insert contact information: email, phone, website URL>

Google Places (including Google Maps, Web Search, and More!)

While the internet may reach around the globe, there are many ways that local businesses can take advantage of the internet in their own backyards. One powerful tool for getting local business exposure online is via Google Places, a free service that makes it easy for users to find your business through Google Maps, Google Web Search, Google Earth, GOOG-411 (phone-based search directory), and Google Maps for Mobile.

Your Google Places listing can include a description of your business, address, phone, website link, hours of operation, photos, coupons, and more. Once your business listing is active, you can log in anytime to find statistics about how many times your listing was displayed in search results, how many people viewed your listing, how many clicked on driving directions, and how many clicked on your website link. You will also see a list of keywords most commonly used to find your listing.

How to Create Your Google Places Listing

1. Go to http://google.com/places.

2. You will need to sign in with your Google account. If you don't yet have one, start by creating your free account.

3. From the Google Places home page, click on "Add New Business." Google will display search results related to your business. If your business is already listed, click on "Edit" to claim the listing and update the information. If no listing exists, proceed with creating your listing.

4. Fill out all of the relevant company details and optional information. Note that Google pays close attention to keywords. When you write the 200-character description of your business, be sure to incorporate relevant keywords that your potential customers might use to find your business. You can also upload photos (including your business logo) and video.

5. Under the Additional Details field, take advantage of the opportunity to add even more information about your business such

as specific services offered, product lines you carry, areas of specialty for your business, etc.

6. Preview your listing and once you are satisfied with it, submit it for publication.

7. Google will require verification for your listing. You can choose to do this by phone (you will receive an automated call with your verification code) or they will send you a postcard in the mail. Once you log in and enter your verification code, your listing will be active and you can make changes and add information as needed.

Once your listing is live, you can post announcements to it from your administration page. For example, you can announce an upcoming event, special sale, or other time-sensitive information. Announcements expire in 30 days. You can also create coupons for your profile anytime.

If you own multiple businesses, Google will actually allow you to create up to 100 listings for free. Optional advertising options are also available for your listing via Google AdWords.

Yelp

Yelp has become one of the top providers of local business listings, making it essential for businesses to create and manage a presence here. This is especially important for businesses that serve a local community since your audience is quite likely to find you here. Yelp's motto is "The power of word of mouth amplified" and its purpose is for users to find and rate businesses through this online directory. With that in mind, you need to create a profile (it's free!) and then collect positive customer reviews.

1. Start here on Yelp: http://www.yelp.com/business

2. You will be asked to search for your business listing. Enter the name of your business and location and view the results. If your business is already listed, be sure to claim it. If not, proceed by clicking on the link to create a business listing.

3. Fill out the basic profile details and submit.

4. You will need to verify your email address by clicking on the link provided in a message sent to you by Yelp. Once this is

complete, you will see a message letting you know that you can claim your listing once it has been reviewed by the Yelp team. In the meantime, click on the link to "Go to Your Yelp Welcome Page."

5. Add photos to your listing, including your business logo and any other photos you want to share with the public.

6. Request reviews from your network. Reviews are very important on Yelp. When consumers are searching for a product or service here, reviews can affect their decisions. Copy the link to your business listing and send it to clients, and share it on your social networks and in your email marketing messages. Consider making review requests an ongoing part of your marketing effort so that you can continue to build up positive feedback over time. If you receive a negative review, the only way to have it removed is to sign up as an advertiser with Yelp. That's right: advertisers can have negative reviews removed.

Superpages

Another online directory for local businesses is Superpages.com. A basic listing is free and it's a good idea to snatch the opportunity to get your business listed in a directory that frequently appears at the top of Google.

1. Go to http://www.superpages.com/about/new_chg_listing.html and click on the link for Business Listing.

2. Superpages searches by phone number. Enter yours to find out if your business is listed. If it is listed, click on the link to claim it. If it isn't listed, continue to add your listing.

3. Fill out profile details and import your company logo and optional photos.

4. Note that you will be asked to purchase paid listings and add-ons. You can click "No Thanks" to bypass these options and claim a free listing.

5. Submit your listing. It will go live within two business days.

Paid Search Engine Placement

Search engine optimization takes time. It could be months before you begin to see results. Depending on the amount of competition you have, it could be difficult to achieve top placement.

If you want to guarantee top placement immediately, pay-per-click advertising is the way to go. Many businesses use a combination of paid placement and SEO strategies to make sure all bases are covered.

Paid or sponsored ads show up at the top of search results and along the right sidebar. When you have a paid ad and your site achieves top placement through SEO efforts, your site will show up several times on the first page, which dramatically improves the chances of reeling in new site visitors.

How It Works

Pay-per-click ads allow you to bid on keywords and phrases by indicating how much you are willing to pay for each *click-through to your site*. Bids can start as low as $.10 each for keyword phrases with very little competition. Popular keyword phrases can cost as much as several dollars per click if there is a significant amount of bidding competition.

For example, you could create an ad campaign for the keyword phrase "personal chef Tampa." If there was little or no competition for this key phrase, your cost would be just a few cents per click. If there were many bidders competing for that phrase, each click could cost you $.50, $1, or more.

Managing Costs and Converting Clicks

The biggest challenges with this type of advertising come from managing costs and converting clicks into customers. As with any marketing investment, the goal is to make the cost of services pay for itself.

So if you bid $.50 per click and 100 visitors click through to your site, your total cost would be $50. Ideally, you want to convert a high percentage of visitors into paying customers. Even if just 2% of your visitors were to make an appointment with you or an online purchase, then the $50 investment would probably be worthwhile for you.

To determine what each customer is worth to you, calculate your average transaction amount (the average sale for a customer at your business) and multiply that by the average number of times a customer spends money with you in a year. The total will be the amount that each new customer is worth to you.

Example:

Average Transaction Fee:	$ 50
Average Transactions Per Year:	x 3
Total Annual Value:	$150

You also have to factor in customer retention. If your customers stay with you for years, the value could be higher. If your customers return just one time, the value could be lower.

Regardless of your budget, none of this will work if you aren't converting site visitors into customers. This gets back to the previous chapters where we discussed the importance of compelling copy on your website, having a call to action, and appealing to your target customers' emotions. When someone visits your website, it should inspire that person to take action.

Note that you can set a daily and/or monthly budget amount for your ads so that you can control how much you invest in ad testing. I recommend testing paid ads with a budget of $100 or more. Give it some time to see if it is effective.

The effectiveness of your pay-per-click ads will depend on whether or not visitors are actually clicking on your ads to begin with. You get a very small amount of space to entice visitors—as few as 25 words—so every word counts. It's a good idea to test different ad copy to see what draws the most response.

Tracking the Results

Determining the success of your pay-per-click campaigns can be measured in a number of ways. Some website owners create special landing pages on their sites for ad-generated traffic. That landing page could have a special code, scheduling tool, or phone number that visitors call to schedule an appointment. You could do something similar for online purchases of gift certificates so that you know when these sales are generated from your ads.

You could also make it part of your standard practice to ask callers how they heard about your business, though this isn't going to be a very accurate measure. It's unlikely that site visitors will know whether or not they clicked on an ad or found your site through an organic search (due to your search engine optimization efforts). Of course, Google will report how many clicks your ad receives based on the budget you set, so you need to find a way to measure conversion rates.

Internet Advertising Providers

According to Comscore.com, as of August 2011 there were 17 billion internet searches conducted per month, and the percentage of searches conducted on each engine looked like this:

Google – 64.8%
Yahoo – 16.13%
Microsoft Sites (Bing, MSN) – 14.7%
Ask — 3%
AOL – 1.3%

Clearly, Google owns the search market; however, it's important to note that paid advertising on the other networks can cost much less due to lack of competition.

Google AdWords

Google AdWords (http://adwords.google.com) is the most popular option for paid search engine advertising because Google owns such a large share of the search market. Google offers a number of advertising options, including pay-per-click results on the main search engine and AdWords for Content.

AdWords for Content will place your ads on other websites that display related ads. For example, a website that features local businesses in your area could feature Google ads that display on the various site pages. If there is an article on the site related to what you do, your ad could get served up based on geography and the topic of the article. This can provide great additional exposure.

Other Search Engines

Yahoo: http://searchmarketing.yahoo.com/
Bing: http://advertising.microsoft.com/search-content-advertising
Ask: http://www.ask.com/products/display
AOL: http://advertising.aol.com/

Getting Help with Pay-Per-Click Advertising

There are service providers who specialize in managing paid search engine placement campaigns. Though you will pay a fee for the luxury of having someone manage this process for you, there can be some big advantages.

These companies should be optimizing your ads on an ongoing basis, producing reports, and evaluating the effectiveness of your ad campaigns. If you have several ads running, a good service provider should be analyzing which ads are doing well and which ads aren't working. They should be adjusting your ads accordingly.

Your web designer may offer these services or be able to refer you to someone who does. You can also check with your chamber of commerce or ask around for a local referral. Because this can all be done virtually, you can hire a service provider located anywhere in the country.

I also suggest that you check contracts carefully and make sure that there is no long-term commitment. Many providers offer services on a month-to-month basis so if someone tries to lock you in to a long-term contract, find another provider.

Monitoring Site Traffic

You're reading this book because you want to improve your online results and to know if your efforts are working, you need to keep track of the results you're getting. Your website hosting provider may offer some reporting features for monitoring traffic. Whether they do or not, Google offers a fantastic free tool with tons of great information: http://analytics.google.com.

Google Analytics provides you with a small piece of HTML code to insert in your website. This allows Google to gather statistics and report your traffic data. Metrics include:

- ❖ Number of visitors to your site
- ❖ Number of page views
- ❖ Average time spent on site
- ❖ Average number of page views

- ❖ Traffic sources (where your traffic is coming from: search engines, links from other sites, direct)
- ❖ Most popular pages
- ❖ Entrance sources (links from other sites leading to your pages)
- ❖ Entrance keywords (keywords used to locate your pages)
- ❖ Percentage change from previous month for various statistics
- ❖ And a whole lot more

The amount of data available here can be overwhelming, but it is quite useful. In particular, you will want to pay attention to the trends over time. If you are consistent in implementing the search engine optimization and content marketing strategies listed in this book, your traffic should show an increase over time. Make a point of reviewing your traffic data each month, and monitor which pages are getting the most traffic. Factor in the links you've shared via social media and other exposure your business has received online.

If for any reason your traffic is not improving within a few months, or worse, it is declining, then something is amiss. Consider hiring an expert to help improve the situation. New competition or other factors can affect your position in the search engines, so it's important to monitor your progress.

It's also difficult to measure the amount of revenue directly generated from your online efforts unless you incorporate special landing pages and methods to track online sales. Ideally, you should see an increase in your overall numbers as time goes on and in alignment with your increase in website traffic and social media participation.

Federal Trade Commission (FTC) Guidelines

If you're promoting anything on your website, you should be aware of the guidelines that were set forth by the FTC in 2009. In a nutshell, the FTC has ordered individuals and businesses to disclose when being paid to promote anything online. In addition, testimonials have come under fire. If you use testimonials on your website, they need to be (1) real, and (2) they cannot over-promise.

The guidelines are overwhelming and frustrating, but you do need to know about them to avoid steep penalties. In most cases, adding a disclaimer to your site and disclosing on social media when you send out a sponsored link are most essential. I'm not an attorney so I can't tell you what to say, but do your homework and make sure you are in compliance.

You can read all the guidelines for yourself at http://www.ftc.gov/os/2009/10/091005endorsementguidesfnnotice.pdf.

Karl Palachuk also wrote two excellent blog posts regarding this topic:

http://blog.smallbizthoughts.com/2010/01/ftc-guidelines-part-one-good-intentions.html and http://blog.smallbizthoughts.com/2010/01/ftc-guidelines-part-two-everyones.html.

Entrepreneur Interview
Name: Roger C. Parker

Business name: Published & Profitable
Website URL: http://www.publishedandprofitable.com
Social media links:

> www.twitter.com/rogercparker
> www.facebook.com/rogercparker
> www.linkedin.com/rogercparker

Tell us about your business and what you do:

My goal is to help businesses and self-employed professionals build their brands by planning, writing, marketing, and profiting from a published book.

Having been involved with publishing and self-employment issues for several decades, I've seen too many first-time authors spend a lot of time writing a book but fail to leverage it to new opportunities and profits.

My goal is to help others avoid making the same mistakes over and over again and enjoy an empowering publishing experience.

Through my Published & Profitable, which is a membership-supported site, I offer more than 500 pages of resources like articles, checklists, examples, inspiring author interviews, templates, tips, and worksheets to help authors jumpstart their book and profit from the experiences of others.

Who is your target audience?

My target audience consists of small service businesses and self-employed professionals who want to write and publish a nonfiction book to be used as a brand-building marketing tool for their business and their career.

How did you get started in your business?

About 20+ years ago, I launched my writing and publishing career by writing a simple (i.e., 72-page) premium book that established my publishing credentials.

Premium books are written for printing and distribution by businesses looking for purchase incentives or, in this case, a reward for software registration.

Within a week of the book's appearance, I was approached by a trade publisher and asked if I was interested in writing an in-depth treatment of the topic. This book, *Looking Good in Print: A Guide to Basic Design for Desktop Publishing*, quickly became a "right-book-at-the-right-time" runaway best-seller.

Looking Good was praised by the *New York Times* and, for more than two years, was the Boston Public Library's most frequently stolen book.

From there, more than 40 other books followed, as well as new client and travel opportunities.

My most successful book, in terms of copies sold, were several editions of my *Microsoft Office for Windows for Dummies*.

What are some of the best tactics you have used to build your audience and establish your authority online?

For several years, I published a monthly newsletter, and promoted it by networking with high-visibility authors in the small business marketing field. For example, for more than a decade I conducted the weekly author teleseminar interviews for Jay Conrad Levinson's Guerrilla Marketing Association.

In addition to online article syndication, I soon turned to blogging several times a week. My original blogs covered all aspects of small business marketing, but I soon began to focus on personal branding issues for self-employed professionals like coaches, clients, and niche marketing for service providers.

For several years, I blogged daily, following a topic-oriented editorial plan, at http://blog.publishedandprofitable.com. I continue to blog several times a week.

How has social media impacted your business? Any success stories you can share?

Blogging and, now, Twitter, is a great way to make friends and build your personal network.

One of my favorite tasks is to blog about books that I've discovered that are relevant to small businesses and self-employed professionals.

Often, I've blogged about new books I've discovered in a local bookstore and received a personal "thank you" email from the author the same day the post appeared! This usually results in a teleseminar interview and establishment of a comfortable, mutually beneficial relationship.

This emphasizes that small-business owners must break out of their shell, and use their writing ability to make new friends and build their network by communicating with the authors who have inspired them and contributed to their success.

For example, in my case, I've been fortunate to interview and spend time with Richard Bolles, author of the yearly best-seller, *What Color Is Your Parachute?*, among others.

Now, of course, the formula is to *leverage my blog* by running RSS feeds from it to my social media outlets, i.e., Facebook and LinkedIn, as well as my author page at Amazon.com.

Do you engage in any communities and if so, how has that impacted your business?

My most successful community-based activity is guest posting on other blogs addressing personal brand building, like Dan Schawbel's Personal Branding Blog, www.personalbrandingblog.com, which has a huge following and is syndicated through hundreds of media outlets.

I also submit articles to other blogs focusing on nonfiction writing, book marketing, and publishing issues.

What role does content play in your marketing strategy?

It's all about content ... sharing helpful, relevant information as concisely and consistently as possible.

Success requires constantly monitoring what's going on in your field and locating new ideas and resources that can help small-business owners build their brand and their profits.

Success is also about developing a voice, or a perspective, that you can constantly build upon while discovering new ideas and techniques that appeal to your interests and passions.

Content success is part investigative—i.e., identifying what your market wants and needs to know—and part following your own nose, exploring ideas that resonate with your passions and interests.

What advice would you offer to readers who want to promote their business online?

The keys to content marketing and brand-building success involve:

- Identifying the market you want to serve, i.e., asking yourself, "Who are my best clients?" and "What are their information needs?"

- Develop the habit of *consistent daily progress*—even if you have only a half-hour a day to devote to marketing your business.

- Create your own deadlines. In addition to scheduling a daily writing session, assign specific goals each day, week, and month. I found it incredibly useful to commit Monday blog posts to planning topics, Tuesday blog posts to writing topics, and Wednesday blog posts to marketing and promotion topics.

- Make the most of everything that you write, so you can reformat and reuse it. This involves creating a system for backing up everything you post online as separate word-processed files. In addition, develop a system for tracking—and easily locating—previously written content saved on your hard drive.

If you were starting your business over today, is there anything you would do differently?

I'd try to locate and partner with someone who shares my passion for clear writing and simple design.

Is there anything else you would like to add?

Life can be great when you love what you're doing, and you've developed the habits, processes, and routines needed to efficiently produce and share your ideas and passions.

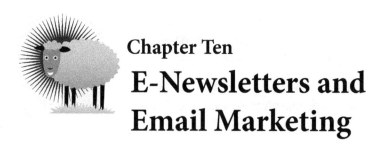

Chapter Ten

E-Newsletters and Email Marketing

"A wise man will make more opportunities than he finds."
—Sir Francis Bacon

E mail marketing can be one of your most valuable tools for promoting your business to your clients and prospects. When someone opts to receive email communication from you, that person is giving you permission to communicate with him or her on a regular basis—an honor you should not take lightly.

It's harder than ever to gain subscribers for a mailing list due to the amount of abuse happening in this space. However, when done correctly, email marketing can have many benefits and a positive impact on your bottom line. Here are some benefits:

Saves Money — Direct mail and print advertisements are expensive and often have a low return on investment. E-newsletters cost just pennies per subscriber and can be significantly more effective.

Proven Response Rate — With direct mail (a sales letter or other printed item sent via postal mail), you are lucky if you get a 5% response rate. According to emailstatcenter.com, the average open rate for electronic marketing is around 23%, click-through rates are 5.9%, and average delivery rate is 96%.

Promotes Your Business with Existing Clients — It costs far less to up-sell to existing customers than it costs to acquire new customers. Email marketing allows you to maintain communications with your customer base and introduce them to new products and services.

Generates Business Leads — When a prospect visits your website and opts to receive your e-newsletter, your newsletter can help convert that lead into a sale.

Shortens Sales Cycles — Industry standards indicate that consumers must be exposed to a product an average of six to eight times before making a decision to buy. An e-newsletter allows you to get repeat exposure with your customers on a regular basis, ultimately improving your sales process.

Builds Customer Loyalty — Studies show that an effective newsletter can bond the reader with the company. By providing quality content in your e-newsletter, you add value for your customers and build loyalty that can last a lifetime.

Improves Professional Image — A professional newsletter elevates your business image and can give you an edge over the competition.

Increases Revenues — A strong call to action along with a special offer, discount, or sale gives newsletter readers incentive to make an immediate purchase.

Creates Immediate Results — Email marketing is timely. You can publicize events, promote new products and services, and announce special sales.

Provides Ongoing Email Marketing Opportunities — Your database of subscriber email addresses can be used for all kinds of promotional purposes. You can send single-page announcements in between newsletters to promote a special sale or event.

Creating an Effective Newsletter

When it comes to planning out your newsletter content, consider the newsletters that you receive. What do you like most? What do you dislike? Evaluating other publications, including those of your competitors, will give you some ideas for how to structure yours.

Give readers a reason to read and keep your newsletter by including a special coupon, industry news, statistics, or useful articles. If you are so inclined, you can even turn your newsletter into an additional revenue stream by selling advertising space to other businesses.

An email newsletter does not need to be flashy. It's more important that it is easy to read and the content is valuable. Include graphic images to give it visual appeal, and use plenty of headlines and bullets to make it easy for readers to scan through your content.

Beware of List Exhaustion

One of the biggest challenges faced with email marketing is keeping your subscribers interested in your messages. If you publish too often or your newsletter does not offer enough value, you will lose subscribers.

The same is true if you send too many promotional messages. It can be tempting to send frequent messages to your entire list to promote various aspects of your business, but if you do this too often, you will begin to exhaust your list. This is part of the churn-and-burn strategy that some internet marketers employ. Though they know they will lose subscribers by sending out frequent messages and sales offers, they don't care because they simply replace those lost subscribers with new ones. You can avoid this fate and earn loyalty from subscribers by respecting your list and limiting the amount of promotional messages that you send out.

Keep an eye on your statistics. A professional e-newsletter service should be able to track how many join your list, unsubscribe, forward your messages, or report you as a spammer. Newsletters with quality content should see a very small percentage of unsubscribe requests, and if you see yours increasing, reevaluate your strategy.

Newsletter Topic Ideas

❖ Articles written by business owner/president

❖ Articles submitted by staff

❖ Articles written by clients

❖ Roundup of recent blog posts

❖ Quick tips (typically a few sentences about something useful)

❖ Resources (website URL's, phone numbers, addresses, etc.)

❖ Advertisements

❖ Frequently asked questions

❖ Greeting from the owner (this is essential to connecting with readers!)

❖ Before and after photos

❖ Contest announcements

❖ Famous quotes

❖ Comic strips

❖ Top-10-type lists ("10 Ways to Fabulous Summer Hair," "12 Reasons Whole Grains Are Good for the Body," etc.)

❖ Masthead (list of contributors)

❖ Business contact information

❖ Industry news

❖ New product/service announcements

❖ Calendar of events

❖ List of contacts

❖ Featured product/service

❖ Coupons

❖ Recipes

❖ Photos

❖ Results of a reader survey

❖ Letters to the editor/feedback from readers

❖ Product reviews

❖ Graphs, tables, or charts

❖ General announcements

❖ Birthdays or anniversaries

- ❖ Historical events/dates
- ❖ Customer profile
- ❖ Testimonials
- ❖ Poem
- ❖ Short story
- ❖ Essay
- ❖ Excerpt from a book
- ❖ Book review
- ❖ Book recommendation

Don't be afraid to promote your products and services within your newsletter. As long as you are providing plenty of useful content, readers will be glad to know about your offers.

Email Deliverability

When you send an email, the recipient's mail host checks your message to determine if it is spam. Guidelines for how these determinations are made vary by provider, but most use a type of ranking system. They look at several factors to "score" the message and determine its probability of being spam.

Following are some general guidelines you can follow to improve deliverability.

1. Avoid using words in the subject line or body of your messages that are commonly used by spammers. Words like "Free," "Credit," "Guaranteed," "Sex," and many others favored by spammers can increase your spam score, especially if there are other elements in the message that also trigger the filters.

2. Using ALL CAPS or excessive punctuation (!!!) in the subject line can affect your score.

3. A blank "To" field (undisclosed recipients) can trigger spam filters.

4. A message that is addressed to dozens of recipients in the "To" field will also hurt your score. Messages should be sent to each recipient individually, which can be accomplished with a professional email marketing service.

Many of the commercial email programs provide tools that allow you to test the spam score for your email messages and alert you to problem areas. When shopping for providers, this is a good feature to look for.

E-Newsletter Service Providers

Sending a newsletter via email becomes challenging as your list grows larger. If you are using an email program such as Microsoft Outlook or AOL mail, the system will likely choke when you attempt to send a message out to several dozen recipients. Spam filters on the recipients' end may also block a large broadcast from being received by subscribers.

Once your list exceeds several dozen subscribers, it's time to invest in a newsletter management system. There are numerous providers to choose from and it costs just pennies per subscriber to manage your email marketing campaigns. Some are even free for up to 500 subscribers.

Providers also offer templates for newsletter design and the ability to set up auto-responders. Auto-responders are used to automate your responses to email or proactively send messages to people on your list. Service providers will also make it easy for you to manage your contact list and will provide HTML code so you can easily add a sign-up box on your website. Here are some popular options:

- ❖ Constant Contact: www.constantcontact.com
- ❖ iContact: www.icontact.com
- ❖ Aweber: www.aweber.com
- ❖ Mail Chimp: www.mailchimp.com

What You Need to Know About the CAN-SPAM Act

The Federal Trade Commission (FTC) is responsible for the CAN-SPAM Act, which includes guidelines for commercial email senders and imposes penalties on those who send messages categorized as spam. To comply with this act, commercial email must adhere to several rules:

1. The "From" and "To" addresses in an email must clearly identify the sender and recipient.

2. The subject line of the message must not be misleading. It should clearly explain what the message is about.

3. All messages must include a way for recipients to opt out of your mailing list. (Once someone opts out, you have 10 days to remove that person from your list.)

4. A valid physical postal address must be included.

In addition to the above rules, commercial email senders cannot harvest email addresses. Unlike direct mail where you can purchase mailing lists, it is illegal to purchase a list of email addresses. Instead, you must build your own list from your customer base by allowing recipients to opt in to your mailing list.

Fines are steep for violating this act—up to $11,000—so it is critical to follow guidelines. For additional details, visit the FTC website: http://www.ftc.gov/bcp/edu/pubs/business/ecommerce/bus61.shtm

Tips for E-Newsletter Success

❖ Encourage new subscribers by making it easy to sign up from every page on your website, and offer some incentive for signing up such as a bonus report, coupon or recording.

❖ Collect newsletter sign-ups from new clients. Make it a practice to ask them if they would like to receive special offers from you via email.

❖ Figure out what your subscribers want to know and earn their loyalty by delivering valuable content.

❖ Never send unsolicited email. Spammers are running rampant in cyberspace and the quickest way to lose customers is to send unsolicited messages. Make sure you get permission from each person on your mailing list.

❖ Beware of spam filters. The algorithms are changing so fast that it's nearly impossible to keep up, but there are certain words that can stop your messages from getting through. Avoid using words like "Free," "Sex," and "Money."

❖ Insert a note encouraging subscribers to "Share this newsletter with a friend."

❖ To comply with current regulations, you should include a link or instructions for customers to unsubscribe to your newsletter.

You shouldn't receive many unsubscribe requests if your content is perceived as valuable.

❖ Remember to include your contact information and website URL in all of your correspondence with customers.

❖ Send promotional announcements sparingly.

❖ Monitor your open rates carefully and pay close attention to your unsubscribe rates and feedback from readers. Email marketing should be closely monitored to best serve your subscribers.

❖ Use compelling subject lines. You want to entice readers to open your message without being misleading about what is inside. Write compelling copy that makes the recipient want to keep reading.

Entrepreneur Interview
Name: Deborah Shames

Business name: Eloqui
Website URL: www.eloqui.biz

Tell us about your business and what you do:

We are presentation specialists, with a focus on innovative business communication. Our firm's name, Eloqui, comes from the Latin "to speak out."

Eloqui training marries performance techniques with the latest research in cognitive science and impression management from the field of psychology. The result is a blend of art and science.

I am a film and television director, while my co-founder David Booth is an actor and corporate spokesman. Together, we have translated performance techniques for business professionals and public speakers.

As experienced trainers with more than a thousand clients, Eloqui works with teams within companies, as well as individual professionals. We identify each person's unique strengths and add targeted skills he or she needs to be effective—everything from identifying an intention, to choosing the right role and techniques for structuring content, to reading an audience and delivering with PowerPoint. The goal is to give our clients the power to communicate with passion, authority, and conviction.

Who is your target audience?

Most companies deliver presentations to clients and customers—whether pitching for new business, delivering performance reports, or motivating their team to improve their numbers. If these presentations receive poor reviews, critical business is at stake. Or, if there is a change event, like a merger or downsize, and a company needs to get everyone on the same page by communicating their messaging, that is when Eloqui training makes the greatest impact.

Our clients include companies as large as Mattel, Fisher-Price, Merrill Lynch, and TD Ameritrade, to smaller law, accounting, financial, and insurance firms throughout the U.S., although we are based in LA.

Across the board, we see companies reducing head count to stay competitive. With the remaining staff, it is even more imperative to focus on their "soft" skills to match their technical expertise. And with enhanced communication and presentation skills, successful leaders are developed from within the organization.

Like corporations, individuals come to Eloqui when they are facing stiffer competition in the marketplace. We frequently hear from our professional clients that they would like to be seen as the "go-to" people in their industry (including being paid for their expertise), have less anxiety when they speak, or advance to the next level in their career.

How did you get started in your business?

For 14 years, I ran Focal Point Productions, a production company based in Sausalito, California, that won more than 60 national and international awards in the entertainment industry. I personally directed luminaries like Danny Glover, Angela Lansbury, Wendie Malick, and Rita Moreno.

Soon after forming Eloqui in Los Angeles, I was voted "Consultant of the Year" by the *San Fernando Valley Business Journal*. I have since coached Hall of Fame athletes, political candidates, entrepreneurs, and many corporate presidents.

David Booth was a classically trained actor on stage and film. In addition to guest starring roles on television, David headed the Advanced Acting Program at PCPA/Solvang, performed at the Oregon Shakespeare Festival, acted in the original ensemble of the Berkeley Repertory Theatre, and was managing director of the Tennessee Williams Center in Key West, Florida.

David represented global companies in the trade show arena throughout the U.S. and Europe, including Cisco, Siemens, and Chevron. David served as spokesman, on-camera narrator, and consultant for hundreds of training videos for banking, technology, energy, and telecommunications corporations. His expertise includes voice-overs and singing, which gives him the ability to repair accents or improve clients' diction.

Together we formed Eloqui—combining our experience from being in front of as well as behind the camera. We are also authors of the best-selling business book *Own the Room: Business Presentations to Persuade, Engage and Get Results*, published by McGraw-Hill in 2009, as well as the *Speaker Survival Guide* and *Briefly Speaking*, which we self-published.

What are some of the best tactics you have used to build your audience and establish your authority online?

Every Sunday morning at 7:30 a.m., Eloqui distributes a speaker tip, quote, and word of the week. When we first started in 2004, we sent out the tip through our email provider, often in small batches. For the last few years, we have used Constant Contact. The Eloqui tip now goes out to more than 3,000 clients, colleagues, and friends, and the response has been overwhelming.

We make sure the tip can be read within about a minute. We also make sure not to "sell" services. Although on occasion we will include a client testimonial, and an announcement of an upcoming public workshop or new project, we are very careful to put these announcements at the end of the tip and make them brief.

Now when we go in to train within a company, network through ProVisors (our business organization), or deliver keynotes around the country, we frequently hear from people who subscribe to our tip. They tell us how they look forward to starting their Sunday morning by reading our tip—over a cup of coffee, on the golf course, or on a hike. Readers forward it on to their colleagues or kids. And they will comment on how the tip reminds them of their own experience, which we love. When the new Eloqui website launches later this year, there will be a blog that expands on the content in the tip and allows for more interactivity.

The most important benefit to Eloqui is the tip keeps us top-of-mind. Frequently, a client we served years ago will reach out to us for a present need and our tip is embedded in their email. And when our book *Own the Room* came out in 2009, readers who wanted to connect with us went to our website and signed up to receive our tip.

How has social media impacted your business? Any success stories you can share?

Although we have business profiles on LinkedIn, we have never been approached by a client who found us through LinkedIn, or the internet for that matter. What *has* been true is that once we've been referred into a company, or submitted a proposal, the potential client has checked out our website and LinkedIn profiles.

I suppose being contacted by Stephanie Chandler for this book could be considered an internet success story. We found this interview opportunity by responding to a request from a reporter (http://helpareporter.com).

Do you engage in any communities and if so, how has that impacted your business?

Our strongest community is ProVisors, a business organization of 1,700+ professionals based primarily in the LA area, but with chapters from San Francisco to San Diego. I lead the Calabasas chapter, while David is a member of Westlake Village. In addition to networking with members and forming strategic alliances, we speak at other groups, focusing on the topics of elevator speeches, constructing compelling client anecdotes, or how to shorten the curve of being considered a trusted advisor.

ProVisors also puts out a weekly email blast, where members can post a need, ask for an introduction into a company, or announce a recent success. This email blast is a great way to stay in touch with professionals you can't logistically see face-to-face.

What advice would you offer to readers who want to promote their business online?

Start a blog. Write a tip. Give away your intellectual property. Then, when you have amassed enough content, write an ebook or deliver a presentation on your area of expertise. Even though you volunteer your time and expertise, you will soon be considered an authority in your field, which will lead to more business and allow you to charge more for the business you presently do.

If you were starting your business over today, is there anything you would do differently?

Eloqui has unique content and satisfied clients who have been very generous in giving us referrals and being available for recommendations. However, if we were starting over, we would assemble a bigger team—with a dedicated sales force, independent contractors as trainers, and more administrative help.

Also, we would make better use of the internet to grow our client base. For example, we could create a mastermind group, charging a subscription fee for access to our resources and consultative services.

Is there anything else you would like to add?

The most satisfying thing about Eloqui is that we have created a forward-thinking firm that positively affects our clients—sometimes profoundly. Steve Jobs suggested that we should all follow our hearts and do something that we love. We couldn't agree more.

Quick Tip

Need a secure place to share or store content online? Check out http://box.net. For automated data backups, see http://backup.ironmountain.com/. To send large files, see http://yousendit.com.

# Chapter Eleven
DIY PR

"If we keep on doin' what we always done, we'll keep on getting what we always got."

—Barbara Lyons

One great advantage of being an authority in your field is that you can become a friend to the media. Print publications, radio, and television all need sources to quote for stories, and industry experts are frequently called upon for interviews.

For example, if there is a breaking news story—such as another politician caught having an affair—marriage therapists and sex experts are brought in to provide their insights. Real estate professionals can comment on the housing market, financial advisors on personal finance, accountants on business finances, pet service professionals on animal issues, and so on.

Getting Media to Come to You

While you can and should pursue media opportunities, you can also position yourself so that media comes to you. Here are some ways to make that happen:

Blog Often – You've already learned how blogging can improve your search rankings, but it can also be a way to attract media. Journalists often use Google to find sources for stories. When you write about topics in your industry and demonstrate your authority, media pros will inevitably find you.

Be Seen in the Right Places Online – The whole premise of this book is to increase your online visibility. When you show up as an authority on other websites, blogs, radio programs, etc., you will attract other media opportunities.

Write a Book – Authors are favorites with media professionals, and they also search Amazon.com for sources. Write that book already!

Get Quoted – One media appearance can lead to another. Publications and programs follow each other's stories, so if you give a great interview in a popular publication or show, there's a good chance you'll get inquiries from others.

Add a Media Page to Your Site — Featuring a media page on your site demonstrates to site visitors that you have a successful business, and it shows the media that you are savvy—making it easier for them to cover you for stories.

Elements of a Media Kit:

A media kit is a collection of information and facts about your business that the media can access to learn about your company. In the past, media kits were traditionally delivered by postal mail in hard-copy format, but access to the internet has led to more and more businesses making their media kits available online. You may include some or all of the following:

❖ Previous media coverage (links to articles, links to media sites, news or radio programs, or a simple list of places where you have appeared)

❖ Company history

❖ Company officers

❖ Press release archives

❖ High-resolution photos

❖ One-page fact sheet about your business

❖ Frequently asked questions with answers (written as if conducted as an interview)

❖ Articles you have authored

❖ Contact information for you or your PR professional

Search-Engine-Optimized Press Releases

Press releases are the long-time standard for generating media coverage. But if you have ever sent out a release, you may know that they can often fall flat and seemingly disappear into a black hole. Press releases can be a hit or a miss, though they can have some other benefits.

Newspapers, magazines, and television news shows use press releases and news tips to locate news and human interest stories. Anyone can send a press release, but to get the attention of reporters, it must be professional, newsworthy, and appealing to the media outlet's target audience.

Press Releases and the Internet

Traditionally, a press release is sent directly to media outlets or sent through a distribution service. One of the most popular online distribution services is http://prweb.com. For a fee, your release can be distributed to hundreds of online news sources, including industry-specific journalists. You can also access press release distribution via http://gebbiepress.com.

Not only can this offer added exposure for your business with the chance of getting featured in a local or national news story, it can also provide some temporary results for search engine optimization and website traffic. Just as you've learned about how to make your website rich in keywords, when you optimize your press release with targeted keywords, you may see some compelling results.

For example, you might issue a press release before Valentine's Day to announce tips for making it romantic. You can use anchored links in your release (text-based links, which are great for SEO) to link back to various pages on your website (the gift certificate page, services page, etc.).

This strategy comes with its share of risks. There are no guarantees that your ranking will increase or that anyone will care about your release. But many businesses report that search-engine-optimized press releases can have an impact on traffic, and if you generate enough business to cover the cost of press release distribution, then it can be worthwhile. Also consider the fact that it only takes one major story to make the effort worthwhile. If your release gets picked up by the *San Francisco Chronicle* or the *New York Times*, that alone can be gold.

How to Write a Press Release

A press release should be brief—just one or two pages—yet include enough details that a reporter could write a short article based solely on the information provided. The release should have an enticing "hook." Good hooks include contests, survey results, industry trends, holiday tie-ins, or awards given or received. The trick is to make the hook interesting enough to capture the interest of a reporter, editor, or producer.

Be careful with your wording to avoid sounding like a sales brochure since that is a quick way to discourage the media from pursuing the story. Follow these rules to write a press release that gets the attention you want:

❖ Read several sample press releases before writing yours so you understand the proper format. Good sources for locating professional releases include www.prweb.com, www.businesswire. com, and www.prnewswire.com.

❖ Start with a proper heading that includes your contact information. When listing phone numbers, indicate a day and evening number (reporters may call at odd hours) or simply list your cell phone number.

❖ Give the release an enticing title that captures the reader's interest, and print it in **ALL CAPS WITH BOLD** type.

❖ Double-space the body of your release for easy reading.

❖ The first paragraph should include the basics of who, what, where, when, and why. You want to lay the foundation and include your hook immediately. Remember that you want to engage your audience and prompt a response from the media.

❖ Determine the purpose of your press release. Is it to announce a special event, introduce a new service, or share valuable information with the public? Include the key points that make your story interesting.

❖ Use quotes from business partners, clients, or other professionals to give the release more credibility. As awkward as it may be, you may want to quote yourself as the owner of the business.

❖ Incorporate keywords and phrases if distributing online.

❖ At the footer of the release, include a brief overview about your business and where it is located.

❖ Do not allow grammar or spelling mistakes to sneak into a press release. Make sure you edit your writing thoroughly and have a friend or trusted staff member review it for errors and content.

❖ If you're unsure about how to write a release, it can be worthwhile to hire an experienced copywriter to help.

To send your press release out locally, start compiling a list of media contacts. Check the websites of your local newspapers, news programs, radio shows, and magazines for contact names and address information. Most media outlets accept press releases by mail, fax, or email, and typically indicate their preferences on the website or publication masthead. If you can't locate press release instructions, it is best to email it directly to the appropriate editor. These days, email is a legitimate format for direct delivery.

Before you send your release, be sure you are prepared to answer interview questions. You may receive calls from reporters immediately and will want to have thoughtful responses ready. Consider writing a list of points you want to make and keep it handy.

Most people find that a press release can be worth its weight in gold when it actually works. A news story usually generates more buzz than any form of paid advertising. Don't be discouraged if your first attempt doesn't receive the attention you want; simply try again until you find the formula and pitch what works.

Reaching Media with Email

Press releases aren't the only way to reach out to media. In fact, I personally favor sending email. Email communication allows you to connect on a more personal level. For most major publications and programs, contact information for reporters, editors, and producers is readily available online.

Years ago, I read a business story in a major publication and took a chance on sending the reporter an email. I introduced myself, complimented the story, and let her know that I was available as a source on several related topics for future stories. She replied and thanked me, saying she would add me to her database.

Several months later, she called me twice in one week and quoted me in stories for Inc.com and the *Los Angeles Times* business section. Over the years she has contacted me repeatedly for stories, all because I took two minutes to send one email.

Don't be afraid to contact media pros directly. Remember that they need sources. Pitch an interesting news topic or add input on a recently covered story and you could find yourself landing in the spotlight.

Fifty Reasons to Contact the Media

1. Comment on industry trend
2. Holiday tie-in
3. Piggyback on breaking news
4. Industry statistics
5. Contest launch
6. Contest results
7. A contest you've won
8. Announce a new product or service
9. Innovative use for your product or service
10. Off-the-wall promotion
11. Special event
12. Comment on news story
13. Charitable contribution
14. Fundraiser you're hosting
15. Fundraiser you're sponsoring
16. Demonstration with broad appeal (i.e., cooking, organizing)

17. Award received
18. Free samples/giveaways
19. Free demonstrations
20. Free classes/events
21. Company anniversary
22. Industry predictions
23. Survey/research launch
24. Survey/research results
25. Alliance/joint venture with another company
26. Tips roundup
27. Release a new white paper or special report
28. Announce new patents
29. Community involvement
30. Partnership with celebrity
31. Open house
32. Company executive to appear at event
33. Incorporation change or IPO
34. New employees or officers
35. Change or launch of board of directors
36. Financial reports
37. Grants you're giving or receiving
38. Scholarships you're giving
39. Sponsorships (i.e., local sports team or Super Bowl)
40. Media coverage received
41. Participation in local events
42. Business expansion
43. Classes or workshops
44. Mergers and acquisitions
45. Take a position on a political issue

46. New location/facilities

47. Authored a book

48. Mentioned in a book

49. Appointment to a board or committee

50. Changes to policies/procedures

Be Prepared When the Media Calls

I sent out my first press release years ago after opening my first business (a bookstore in Sacramento). I didn't know much about what I was doing at the time, so I wrote the release and sent it off to several media outlets. Then I went to the mall.

My phone rang while I was in the dressing room at Macy's. It was a reporter who was prepared to interview me on the spot. I sat down and as we chatted, I realized that I was completely unprepared. I hadn't anticipated her questions and therefore, I fumbled my answers.

Since then, I've been through professional media training to learn tricks of the trade. Now I understand the importance of being prepared, knowing what points I want to get across, and methods for steering an interview back to the topic at hand.

The reality is that whether you contact the media or not, there's a good chance they will call you at some point, especially if you use the strategies from this book! Here are some tips so you can be prepared when the media calls:

1. Anticipate questions. Write them down and develop a list of bullet points for each that cover details you want to mention.

2. Know what messages you want to convey. Though you might end up answering questions for 15 minutes, it's likely that only a few quotes will end up in the story. Every comment counts, so make sure each answer you give has impact.

3. For radio and TV, there's little or no editing. Everything you say is recorded for all eternity. All the more reason to know your key messages, practice them, say them out loud in the car, have your kids interview you at the dinner table—whatever it takes to be ready.

4. Talk in sound bytes. The media likes short answers that are to the point, especially on radio and TV. Questions come in rapid-fire fashion and your answers should keep up with the pace. If your answers drag on during a live TV interview, you can bet that you won't be invited back.

5. Be available for at least a week after sending out a press release. Don't go on vacation or disappear for several days. If a reporter calls and leaves a message, call back as soon as humanly possible. There are always deadlines involved. I learned this one the hard way when my son was home sick and I failed to check voice mail until the next day. I missed a great opportunity to be quoted in a national business magazine.

6. Have fun with interviews. You want to be prepared without sounding like a robot. Let your personality shine through and make the reporter's job easy. When you're a good interview subject, there is a good chance you will be contacted by that reporter again in the future. The reporter who interviewed me while I was at the mall still calls on me year after year—despite the fact that I was unprepared—all because I managed to have a sense of humor during the interview.

7. Thank the reporter after the interview. Reporters do not get enough appreciation for what they do and when you take time to send a quick note, it will be noticed and remembered. Reporters need a lot of sources and they are people, too. Show that you are a great source and you can build a relationship that endures.

Resources for Additional Media Coverage

Help a Reporter Out (HARO) is a free service that you can subscribe to and receive three daily emails with requests from reporters. Monitor this service closely and respond directly to reporters when your expertise fits their requests. Note that you can also use HARO as a reporter to find guests for your radio show or podcast or to solicit interviews for blog content, books, or articles. http://helpareporter.com

ProfNet is an online community for professionals (authorities!) to list their areas of expertise. Reporters come for free to find sources, while as a contributor you will pay to get listed. http://profnet.com

Entrepreneur Interview
Name: Maria Nemeth, Ph.D., MCC

Business Name: Two businesses: Academy for Coaching Excellence and Maria Nemeth, Ph.D., coaching and consulting.
Website URL: www.marianemeth.com

Social media links:

> http://www.facebook.com/marianemethph.d
> https://twitter.com/maria_nemeth
> http://www.linkedin.com/pub/maria-nemeth/12/358/b27

Tell us about your business and what you do:

At the Academy for Coaching Excellence, we offer training to such varied groups as government employees, financial planners, educators, physicians, corporate leaders, and mental health counselors who see the value that cutting-edge coaching skills would bring to their profession. In addition, we are accredited through the International Coach Federation to provide professional, internationally recognized certification for those who wish to become life or executive coaches. We also offer programs for those who are looking for personal development that will show them how to bring clarity, focus, ease, and grace to life. We have a center in Sacramento as well as Stockholm, Sweden. We work with private as well as governmental groups.

In my private business, I coach individuals, groups, and teams wishing to be successful at achieving meaningful goals.

Who is your target audience?

That's a good question. At the Academy, we see people who are at an important crossroads. This could be someone who is 23 and just getting into the workforce and wants coaching skills for a future job, or someone 35-55 who wants to develop a second career and thinks coaching might just fill a need to empower others to be successful. But what's crucial is that the person is willing to question his or her most closely held personal assumptions about human potential. We are all capable of achieving what is most meaningful for us. What stops us is our belief that it isn't possible. And coaching is all about learning to navigate around our self-limiting internal conversations.

For myself in the coaching and consulting business, I see clients who live around the world. A young business executive in Shanghai, an entrepreneur in Sacramento, a teacher in east Los Angeles, a government worker in India, a corporate coach in Stockholm, a financial advisor in the U.K., and a hospital administrator in the Midwest—these are examples of people I coach. I also work with teams who want to maximize their strengths so as to make the best use of resources to produce extraordinary results.

How did you get started in your business?

I am a clinical psychologist by training. I have taught at the university level and have had a full-time private practice as a psychotherapist. One thing kept emerging: after people had worked through conflicts, issues, and crises, there were always questions. They went something like this: "Now that all is well, how will I live the rest of my life?" "What do I want to accomplish?" "What is really important to me?" Psychology couldn't answer those questions as fully as I would have liked. Instead, I learned about coaching and what a well-trained coach does. A coach is someone who creates an environment in which people can see what they want to accomplish with their lives. The coach also supports them to go past the point where they would normally give up on themselves or their dreams. Coaching is a very optimistic, proactive profession. I was hooked!

What are some of the best tactics you have used to build your audience and establish your authority online?

I have relied upon the support of others who know much more about building audiences than I do. So much of the time, we think we have to possess knowledge and mastery in skills that have nothing to do with our profession. We end up being mediocre because we are not meant to do everything perfectly. In fact, people who are truly successful in life surround themselves with others who have the requisite knowledge, skill, or capability to support them in achieving the goals that are important.

And, I also prefer not to think about establishing my authority online so much as establishing my *value* online. Today's e-commerce is based upon relationship and value. That's what keeps it so fresh.

How has social media impacted your business? Any success stories you can share?

Last month, I found out that I'd been given this award as one of the 50 most influential people in the U.K. in the field of financial advice. Now, I'm not a financial advisor. However, I've been working with advisors in how to talk with clients about money and how to create trust. Because I have a social media platform, we were able to get this out to a large group of people who might otherwise not have known about my work.

What is the success in this? The success involves the exchange of information with a group of people who are now interested in hearing more about what I do since the social media broadcast. Where will it lead? I truly don't know. However, continual communication and engagement are what bring about opportunities. And this is what interests me the most: engagement and the opportunity to make a difference in the lives of people. So, ask me this question again in a year or so and I'll tell you where it all led.

Do you engage in any communities and if so, how has that impacted your business?

No, I do not, at present, engage in any communities. I am looking at doing this in the near future as a way to build relationships.

What role does content play in your marketing strategy?

I have written three books. The middle one, *The Energy of* Money, got me on the *Oprah Winfrey Show*. Talk about a marketing moment! It was a joy to be there. It didn't heavily impact book sales. However, it has given me some professional standing and has opened doors to speak in front of people all around the world. I write short articles called "Luminous Letters" that people can get once they go to my personal website. We are also in the finishing stages of a DVD called *The Energy of Money* that will be marketed worldwide. And I am putting into place a system for short videos, available weekly on my website, which will give people something to think about in terms of their personal success. The bottom line is this: Content is where people learn about your approach and what you think. It creates relationship.

What advice would you offer to readers who want to promote their business online?

Find partnerships that allow you to link to the websites of those who share your approach or values. Strive to give first. People love that. Make it compelling for folks to visit your website at least once a month. Be in it for the long-haul. What pays off most of all is persistence.

If you were starting your business over today, is there anything you would do differently?

I would have gotten into online business promotion sooner. I would have offered free content more quickly. When I first started seeing people as a coach—back when Lincoln was president—online business was for folks who sold vitamins and facial products. And, come to think of it, when I first opened the Academy for Coaching Excellence 10 years ago, we didn't have a fraction of the internet opportunities that we have today.

So, I guess my answer is I would have waited 10 years until the internet was more developed before doing any business. The trouble is, hindsight is always 20/20, isn't it? We simply have to jump in at some point. And that's what I've done. And if I have done it, I guarantee that anyone can do it!

Is there anything else you would like to add?

Ask yourself these questions:

- Would it be OK with me if life got easier?

- Would it be OK with me to discover there's nothing wrong with me, my ideas, or my dreams?

- That all I need is to allow myself to create generative relationships with people who can do some things better than I can?

Chapter Twelve

Internet Revenue Streams

"The world stands aside to let anyone pass who knows where he is going."

—David Starr Jordan

If you're going to invest time, money, and effort into boosting your visibility online, then it makes sense to also increase your revenue streams. Who doesn't want to make more money? I have dozens of revenue streams, which adds financial security and a steady increase to my earnings each year. This chapter covers several ways that you can generate more revenues online.

Google AdSense

One of the fastest and easiest ways to add a new revenue stream is with Google AdSense: www.adsense.google.com. This service allows you to place advertisements on your website or blog and get paid whenever someone clicks on an ad. Ads can be text-based or image-based, with a variety of sizes and formats to fit your needs. Google also serves up smart advertising by matching the content of the ads with the content on your site. So if you have an article about how to bake a cake, the resulting ads might come from cookbook sites, cooking sites, and other related offers.

Several years back when BusinessInfoGuide.com was growing, I was hesitant to put ads on the site. I didn't want the site to look like an ad farm or for the ads to distract from the value of the content. I eventually decided to test out the ads by placing them on about a dozen pages.

As soon as I saw the revenues earned from those ads, I realized that I could still offer great content while also getting paid for those efforts.

Today, the site features a variety of AdSense ads and my only regret is that I didn't add them sooner! This is a significant revenue stream that automatically places money in my bank account each month. Depending on the amount of site content and traffic to your site, you can earn hundreds or even thousands of dollars from these ads. And because so many websites earn their revenues from advertising, site visitors have grown accustomed to seeing these types of ads online.

Though AdSense is the clear leader for site ads, other options to consider include http://kontera.com, http://chitika.com, http://adbrite.com, and http://doubleclick.com. You can also sell ads directly to companies for placement on your site. One service that helps you manage this process is http://buysellads.com.

Affiliate Sales

Joining affiliate programs allows you to earn money from your website by recommending other products. For example, if you recommend a computer for sale through Best Buy, and a site visitor clicks through the link or banner ad and purchases the computer, you earn a percentage of the sale.

Many businesses offer affiliate programs and to be successful, you should match up products and services that meet the needs of your target audience. Note that you can also create your own affiliate programs and pay others a commission to sell your products and services.

Following are sites that offer affiliate programs:

CommissionJunction.com – This site allows you to sign up for affiliate programs for more than 1,000 companies, including eBay, HP, Verizon, Yahoo, and many others.

LinkShare.com – This is another merchant that allows you to set up affiliate accounts with many big merchants, including Dell, 1-800-Flowers.com, Cingular, Chase, and more.

Associates.Amazon.com – Sell books and other products through Amazon.com. You can generate product images, banner ads, text links, and more. If you're already recommending books, you might as well get paid for it. As a bonus, Amazon doesn't just pay you for the books users buy; it pays a percentage based on the entire contents of their shopping carts when they check out.

PayLoadz.com – Create your own affiliate programs for electronic products such as ebooks or MP3 files, or sell affiliate products listed in their product store.

PayDotCom.com — Allows you to set up your own affiliate programs for your products so others can resell them.

1ShoppingCart.com and e-junkie.com – Both offer a robust online shopping cart solution and the ability to create your own affiliate links for your products, or create affiliate links to sell other people's products.

ClickBank.com – An enormous directory of information products where you can become an affiliate and promote other people's products or make your own products available.

CafePress.com – You can design your own merchandise such as t-shirts, mugs, license plate frames, and mouse pads, and then earn money from every sale.

Zazzle.com – Similar to CafePress, Zazzle allows you to design your own products ranging from t-shirts to speakers and sell them for a commission.

Information Products

We have previously explored information products for marketing purposes, though they can also be a source of revenue for all kinds of businesses. Information products can come in any of the following formats:

- ❖ Books
- ❖ Ebooks
- ❖ Special Reports
- ❖ White papers
- ❖ Webinars

- ❖ Teleseminars
- ❖ Podcasts
- ❖ Videos
- ❖ Workbooks
- ❖ A bundle of any of the above
- ❖ Any other way that you can compile and sell information

I have been selling a variety of info products for years. Most recently, I hired a team to research and compile lists of internet radio shows that we sell to business owners and authors who want to pitch themselves for interviews. Since I used to own a bookstore and was constantly asked how others could do the same, I wrote a workbook on how to start and run a used book store. Because the workbook has been one my top-selling products for years, I converted it to trade paperback and now sell it through Amazon, BN.com, and other online retailers. I also sell recordings to online classes and seminars that I've hosted, plus ebook versions of my books and a variety of special reports.

Not only can information products generate additional revenue, they can attract new customers for your business. With every product you create, you have a new reason to reach out to your audience.

How to Generate Ideas for Information Products

1. Teach Your Audience

To begin the brainstorming process, make a list of everything you know how to do. For example, if you are a career coach, you probably know how to write a killer résumé, how to prepare for an interview, what to avoid saying during the interview process, what you should say during the interview process, how to dress for success, etc. The list of topics you create can become ideal products for your target audience.

2. Find Out What Your Audience Wants and Needs

It doesn't make any sense to develop a product unless you know you have an eager audience ready to buy. Ask your audience for product ideas via your newsletter or social media.

You can also get great feedback by conducting a survey. See http://surveymonkey.com to easily create an online survey.

3. **Pay Attention to Questions You Are Asked Most Frequently**

   Often times, this can be the key to creating a high-demand product, as was the case with the bookstore workbook I created. Online business manager Sharon Broughton found herself constantly answering questions about how to set up online shopping carts. In response, she developed a series of online training courses that converted into self-study courses. This was a smart way to leverage information products and add a revenue stream for her business.

4. **Use What You Already Have**

   Compile your best articles or blog entries and turn them into white papers, or take topics from your existing book and expand them into short reports. Also, look at the databases you keep and ask whether people would be willing to pay for them. Years ago when the article marketing craze was happening, I began selling my own personal list of 100+ websites that accepted article submissions, which I eventually expanded to 600+ websites. It sold like crazy.

5. **Learn Something New and Share**

   I believe that to be the best in your field you should always be learning. So go figure out how to do something, master it to the best of your ability, and then teach others what you've learned. For example, an artist might teach a class on a new art medium or technique.

Examples and ways to generate ideas for information products:

❖ If you've created a spreadsheet for tracking sales leads or monitoring your business or just about anything else that your audience would find useful, sell it as a pre-formatted template.

❖ Compile a list of media contacts for your industry and turn it into a directory.

❖ Compile a white paper that includes the latest statistics for your industry.

❖ If you've had success with antiques, collectibles, electronic products, homemade goods, or anything else on eBay, help others understand what worked.

❖ Tell your story: "How I took $500 and built an amazing business, and how you can, too!"

❖ Create an anthology. Contact others in your field and ask them to contribute an article or essay.

❖ Compile your articles or blog posts into a book or ebook.

❖ Show how to start a business in your industry. Include sample forms and worksheets that you use in your daily business operations.

❖ Compile articles that you have written and create exercises for each one to create a workbook that you can sell in print or PDF format.

❖ Show how you did something and then include an outline for the reader to do it, too. For example, you could explain how you marketed your business over a three-year period and then include an outline for a marketing plan, with room for the reader to fill in his own details.

❖ Develop a companion workbook that the audience follows through while you give a presentation.

❖ Conduct a weekly class via teleseminar, webinar, or email, and have students send back homework for you to review. Sell the recordings and materials after the course is complete.

❖ Offer daily exercises for a period of time. For example, "60 Days to Natural Living."

❖ If you have contracts, forms, or procedures for your business, sell them as individual templates or compile a series of them into one bundle.

50 Ways to Transform Content into Information Products

Following is a list of products to give you more ideas for what you can create.

1. Books
2. Mini-books (they don't all have to read like novels!)
3. Booklets
4. Ebooks
5. Special reports
6. White papers
7. Workbooks
8. Worksheets
9. Templates
10. Resource lists
11. Database of resources
12. Spreadsheets
13. Pre-formatted spreadsheet templates
14. Charts/graphs
15. Checklists
16. Statistics
17. Survey results
18. Blog posts
19. Articles
20. Case studies
21. Interviews
22. Compilations (stories, articles, interviews, case studies, etc.)
23. Videos (full-length)
24. Video clips
25. Video trailers

26. Audio recordings

27. Audio recording series

28. Podcasts

29. Teleseminars

30. Teleseminar series

31. Webinars

32. Webinar series

33. Transcripts

34. E-newsletters

35. Print newsletters

36. Print magazines

37. Web-based magazines

38. Comic strips

39. Games

40. Card decks

41. Short stories

42. Computer-based training

43. Email auto-responder series

44. iPhone apps

45. iPad apps

46. Sample chapters

47. Audio books

48. Licensed content (articles, graphics, etc., that others can repurpose)

49. Ring tones

50. Bundles (collection of several items listed above)

You can download a printable version of the above list at http://businessinfoguide.com/wp-content/uploads/50-Ways-to-Transform-Content-into-Information-Products.pdf. Also, I wrote an entire book on this topic, which you can find in most bookstores: *From Entrepreneur to*

Infopreneur: Make Money with Books, eBooks and Information Products (John Wiley & Sons).

Online Events

We covered teleseminars and webinars for marketing purposes in the Content Marketing chapter, but now we'll discuss how to create profitable online events. I have used the teleseminar format in numerous ways over the years. I've held a number of free events as a way to attract new prospects and gather contact information. I've also used this format for hosting classes.

For example, I held an eight-week marketing course for authors via a weekly one-hour teleseminar. I delivered it in lecture format, allowed participants to ask questions at the end, and I even assigned homework. Not only did this attract new prospects, it was a profitable venture thanks to the students who attended live and those who purchased the recordings after the course was over.

I also held a nonfiction writers' conference in 2010, conducted entirely via teleseminar. It included 18 speakers over three days. Each gave an hour-long lecture on a specific topic.

The conference involved a tremendous amount of work to put it all together, invite speakers, coordinate details with them, write the sales copy, promote the event, handle registrations, conduct the actual calls for three straight days, have everything transcribed, and set up a shopping cart. I couldn't have done it without the help of a savvy assistant who was much better at detail-oriented work than I am! In the end, it was a profitable venture that attracted new clients, allowed me to connect with some top authorities when I invited them to speak, garnered some media coverage from *Writer's Digest* magazine, and resulted in a set of 18 recordings that I continue to sell online.

I have always wondered why more people don't conduct classes or conferences online. It allows you to reach an audience around the globe and can be quite lucrative. Yes, there can be some work involved, especially if you hold a large event, but there's work involved in just about anything that is worthwhile!

Event Planning Guidelines

1. **Write Sales Copy** – Who do you want to attend and what are the benefits to them? Write your sales copy, complete with attendee benefits. Don't bother with cheesy testimonials from people you know. If you've held similar events in the past, you can include testimonials from actual attendees. Manufactured testimonials from your online "friends" rarely do much to impress. No sleazy sales tactics are needed, though you do need to ask for the sale. In fact, there's a good chance you'll get more sign-ups if your online sales page DOESN'T resemble those long-form "But wait, there's more!" sales pages.

   You will also need to write copy for your email messages to your audience, social media engagement, and follow-up copy. Prepare as much as possible in advance so you will be ready to go when needed.

   Note that your event may simply need a page on your site or may require a separate website altogether—your choice. In addition to sales copy, you should include some images to break it up and give more visual appeal. Include your photo and others that represent the content you are offering. If you have guest speakers, they should provide photos and bios for display on the site.

2. **Plan Your Pricing** – If you're going to include early-bird pricing (and you probably should), make a plan for what that looks like and when it will be offered.

3. **Create a Planning Calendar** – Ideally, you should create a calendar with dates for different prices you will offer, along with plans for when you will send announcements to your email list, social networks, affiliates, etc. Your whole marketing plan should be factored into your calendar to make sure you stay on top of the event. You can find free printable calendar pages online.

4. **Set Up Your Shopping Cart** – Please, please, please don't ask attendees to register via email or call you! This is a big barrier

to entry. If you want to fill your event, make online registration as easy as possible. You can use something as simple as PayPal, or a more sophisticated shopping cart solution such as www.e-junkie.com.

Another option I love is www.eventbrite.com. This service handles all of the registration details, including payment processing, email to attendees, and more. Note that for free events Eventbrite is free to use, but for paid events they will charge a service fee that you can either charge to your buyers or absorb into your costs. I recommend absorbing it into costs to remove another potential sales barrier.

5. **Choose Your Service Provider** – Before you launch your event, do your homework and know which platform you are going to use to deliver the event. For teleseminars and online conferences, my favorite solution is www.instantteleseminar. com. For webinars, consider www.gotomeeting.com or www. webex.com. Check pricing and recording options before your event and if you haven't used the service before, stage a practice session so you can learn how it works.

6. **Invite Affiliates** – If you have a network of people who would be interested in selling seats to your event, then go ahead and ask if they would like to earn a commission on any sales generated. Also, if you have guest speakers for your event, an incentive for them to participate could be earning a percentage of any sales they refer your way. Affiliate commissions range from 10% to 50%, though the more you pay the more incentive others will have to promote it for you. While it may be hard to imagine giving away half of your profit, consider that you're actually earning more for attendees that you wouldn't otherwise have.

For affiliates, you will need to write the copy that invites them to participate. You should also make things easy for them by writing up sales copy they can use in their blogs, newsletters, and social media. That means writing a variety of versions from several paragraphs down to a 140-character tweet. To run an affiliate program, you will need to use a more sophisticated shopping cart solution such as 1shoppingcart.com or e-junkie.com.

7. **Develop Content and Scripts** – For the actual delivery of your event, class, conference, or whatever you are doing, you will need to prepare content and scripts. A script should be used to open and close the session to make sure you sound polished and include any important details—like where attendees can go to download a handout or how they can mute or unmute their phone lines. Of course, you should introduce yourself since not everyone may know much about you, and always mention your website and places where attendees can get more information.

   If you are delivering your session in lecture-format, prepare your training materials well in advance. I personally like to create a topic outline with key points that I want to get across. I never script it word-for-word because I want to deliver it naturally, though if a script is more comfortable for you, by all means create one. I also like to plan for more content that I think I will need just in case there is time left over. I always have bonus topics handy.

   If you're introducing guest speakers, you will need to read their bios out loud. Ask the speakers to provide the bios so that you don't butcher their information or pull details that are outdated.

8. **Promote, Promote, Promote** – If you want people to attend your event, you need to invite them—and then remind them repeatedly. You should begin promoting well in advance—ideally at least 60 days ahead of time (though 30 days can work if you're aggressive with promotion).

   Of course, you still have to ask for the sale, and providing some incentive is a good idea. Early-bird discounts are standard practice. You can also give away some bonuses for attendees such as a workbook, handouts, or a downloadable ebook.

Get creative! The more unique your event and its benefits, the more likely you will attract interest.

Start by sending an initial event announcement out via your newsletter and social media networks. Be sure to include a big early-bird discount of 30% to 50% off and a link to the registration page. You can also feature the event on the home page of your website and via any trade associations that you belong to. See if you can announce your event in their next newsletter.

Repeat announcements on social media networks often. For email, I'm not a fan of sending frequent communications. At the same time, you do need to remind people to register and expose them to the event several times before they make a decision (especially if your price point is high). Don't abuse your email list, but do leverage it for event promotion. Pay close attention to your response rate and unsubscribe rates, too.

If your event is a bigger-ticket item, you may want to offer a free preview call. Invite potential attendees to learn about the event and ask questions. Better yet, hold a free educational teleseminar loosely based on topics from your event. Offer up some great content and then close with a special offer to attend your event.

9. **Hire Some Help** – If you're coordinating a smaller event, you're the only speaker, and you're comfortable with all of these details, then go forward and prosper! But if this sounds overwhelming to you or you have multiple speakers, consider hiring an experienced virtual assistant to help with your event. Remember that you will also need to make sure your event sessions are recorded, recordings need to be download and made available for sale after the fact, and you may also want to have them transcribed. All of this requires even more work! The International Virtual Assistants Association (www.ivaa.org) has a directory of providers to choose from, as does www.assistu.com.

Paid Content

There are an increasing number of websites that allow contributors to earn money from contributing content. These can generate additional exposure for users and their content while also generating revenue. Squidoo (www.squidoo.com), which is hosted by Seth Godin and friends, allows users to create a "lens," which is essentially like an individual blog post. Squidoo touts its high page rank in Google as a way for contributors to generate traffic.

Squidoo offers revenue sharing for its participants. Because the site is ad-supported, contributors receive half of the profits generated from ad links. Savvy Squidoo users seek out top keywords and write content around those keywords to capitalize on top placement in the search engines and the ad revenue that is generated as a result of the traffic.

HubPages (www.hubpages.com) is similar to Squidoo, allowing users to generate content and enjoy ad revenue sharing from Google Ads, Kontera, Amazon, and eBay. Another option is Associated Content (www.associatedcontent.com), which is a Yahoo!-owned company that touts itself as "The world's largest source of community-contributed content." Here writers get paid based on the traffic generated by articles. There is also an assignment desk where you can pick up paid assignments. Top contributors get more visibility on the site.

If you're interested in taking on a role as expert and content contributor, look to www.about.com. This site is loaded with topics from parenting to gardening and everything in between. Content guides must apply for the exclusive position of representing a topic, and then create and acquire content for that topic, plus send emails to followers.

I'm not going to tell you that you'll get rich from these sources, but if you're prolific and want to give them a try, you can generate some additional income and gain some visibility, too. Here are some other sites to investigate. Each has various compensation plans ranging from advertising revenue share to paying per post.

- ❖ www.helium.com
- ❖ www.ehow.com
- ❖ www.lovetoknow.com

- ❖ www.sponsoredreviews.com
- ❖ www.docstoc.com
- ❖ www.daytipper.com
- ❖ www.examiner.com
- ❖ www.flixya.com
- ❖ www.reviewparty.com
- ❖ www.bloggerparty.com
- ❖ www.xomba.com
- ❖ www.triond.com
- ❖ www.blogvertise.com
- ❖ www.wisebread.com
- ❖ www.wiretapmag.com
- ❖ www.reviewme.com
- ❖ www.smorty.com
- ❖ www.payperpost.com

Along these same lines, if you're active on Twitter, you can get sponsorship for tweets. Check out www.sponsoredtweets.com, where celebrities generate big bucks for a single tweet, and industry experts with a decent following can also get paid.

Entrepreneur Interview
Name: Al Lautenslager

Business name: Market For Profits
Website URL: http://www.marketforprofits.com, http://www.re-the-book.com

Social media links:

> http://www.facebook.com/allautenslager
> http://www.twitter.com/gmarketingguy
> http://www.linkedin.com/in/allautenslager

Tell us about your business and what you do:

I am a speaker, best-selling author, and marketing consultant. I also am an adjunct instructor at two colleges in Wisconsin, one at the MBA level.

Who is your target audience?

Small- to medium-size-business owners, professionals of all kinds, nonprofit groups; any organization that wants to build or reinvent a business, or people that want to reinvent themselves.

How did you get started in your business?

With a corporate marketing background, and as a business owner for 15 years, I was always being asked to help others through consulting or speaking, so I turned both into businesses. Now that, plus book publishing, plus teaching, is what I focus on.

What are some of the best tactics you have used to build your audience and establish your authority online?

Networking, PR, and direct email; practicing what I preach; speaking to anybody and everybody; relentless marketing; always leveraging and an integrated approach; thinking marketing all the time. Tying myself to a media story and getting even more PR. All of these usually have an online tie-in that positions me—creates Google Juice and general awareness along with all the offline marketing that I do. Integration is a repetitive theme here.

How has social media impacted your business? Any success stories you can share?

I did a ten-day speaking/book-signing tour in Southeast Asia in 2010 that came as a result of a meeting planner seeing a conversation I was having on Facebook about me speaking and helping business owners. I also started a social media training company to help me leverage all the marketing that I do, whether it is consulting or speaking or book related. www.certifiedsocialmedia.com was started with Kurt Scholle of www.webasylum.com to help others leverage this part of their marketing plan in a total integrated marketing approach. People still comment to me, "I see you everywhere." I'm not everywhere, but I happen to be where my target market is looking, and I purposely engage and participate in the respective communities that accomplish that. I am always announcing where I am speaking, who I am visiting, what projects I am working on, related links to stories about what I speak about, all generally positioning my expertise while at the same time sharing information with my communities. I therefore am a resource of value, many times the "go-to" person for the things I am an expert in.

Do you engage in any communities and if so, how has that impacted your business?

Many LinkedIn groups (they allow 50 and I am at the max), National Speakers Association, and local networking groups.

What role does content play in your marketing strategy?

Articles I have written that are online stay online. I have many at www.entrepreneur.com that preceded the publishing of my books with Entrepreneur Media, the publisher of *Entrepreneur* magazine. I am now blogging for the new book *RE*: www.RE-the-book.com. I have also had much luck being asked to guest blog on many marketing-related sites. My books are lead-generators for speaking and consulting in a big way. I call them my $22 brochures.

What advice would you offer to readers who want to promote their business online?

Use an integrated approach. Marketing is made up of many, many, many, many things—even online. Use the communities you participate in. Engage in conversation. Make relationships. Meet online connections offline (this one is huge). Get attention, make people remember, and then make them talk about you or your business (buzz).

If you were starting your business over today, is there anything you would do differently?

I would do all of my entrepreneurial ventures earlier—maybe focus more, but I do like the general approach to many streams of income. I would connect with more who have done what I want to do in mentoring situations if I could, and I would start writing much, much earlier.

Is there anything else you would like to add?

Do not confuse activity with progress. Think every day how you can make more income, meet more people, leverage all of your activity, while making a profit. From a marketing perspective think, "How am I building the awareness of my products and services with my prospects and customers?" I think about this mindset every single day. As Henry Ford says, whether you think you can or can't, you're right.

Chapter Thirteen

Build Your Audience Offline

"Have the courage to follow your heart and intuition. They somehow already know what you truly want to become."
—Steve Jobs

While this book is primarily about building your business and your audience online, there are some important offline strategies I want to address as well. These days, the majority of businesses need both online and offline marketing strategies to stay competitive. Following are more tactics for leveraging your authority, sharing content, and building an audience that wants to buy your services and products.

Professional Speaking

Though it may be among people's top fears—next to the fear of flying and ahead of the fear of death—public speaking has many advantages. As the featured speaker at an event, conference, or meeting, you are perceived as the ultimate authority in the room. Speakers have a tremendous amount of influence with an audience, which removes a great barrier from purchasing your services. Speaking also allows you to reach large numbers of people. For example, a trade association with 600 members may only get 60 people to attend the meeting, but as the speaker your information and bio are promoted to all 600 members.

There are dozens, if not hundreds, of trade organizations in every major city that need speakers for their weekly or monthly meetings. That's right, they NEED speakers. As someone who has been in charge of running numerous groups in my community over the years, it is always difficult to find speakers because not enough people make an effort to reach out. That equals opportunity for you!

In addition to trade associations, consider teaching at your local adult learning centers and community education programs. Even if only 10 students register for your class, your business is promoted in their catalog, which is often sent to tens of thousands of people. Other potential venues include retirement centers, community centers, churches, schools, and charitable organizations.

Here are the steps to getting on the speaking circuit:

1. Write a brief and interesting description of your presentation and what attendees will learn. If you're inclined, you can also develop several presentation topics.

2. Add a Speaker page to your website. Include a description of your topics and any testimonials that you gather from your engagements. This effort alone can bring opportunities, especially when combined with your other efforts to optimize your site for search engines.

3. Contact local trade associations, groups, schools, and organizations *that reach your target audience* and let them know that you are available to speak. You should be able to find contact information on websites and can simply send an email to introduce yourself.

4. Pack your presentation with useful information. *Do not make it a sales pitch for your business!* If the audience likes what you have to say, they will want to learn more about you and your business. Make it educational, funny, interesting, and engaging. Use plenty of stories and examples. Practice it several times out loud, even if it's just in front of your cat, to make sure it flows well.

5. Engage the audience by asking questions and soliciting their participation.

6. Use props, when appropriate, for visual interest. But don't use gimmicky props! I once watched a business speaker juggle

scarves. It didn't fit the theme of the presentation, was distracting, and left the entire room looking a little uncomfortable. On the other hand, visual props that illustrate a point can enhance your presentation. I always bring along examples when I speak about information products and then I pass them around the room.

7. Give attendees something to keep such as a single-page handout with tips or a booklet. Be sure to include your company contact information. Remember, brochures are boring. The goal is to give them something that they will keep handy to remember you later.

8. Respect the time allotted. It's better to finish early than late—then you can open the floor for questions. When you run over your time, you risk losing the audience's attention, especially if they are anticipating a break.

9. Wrap up with a brief pitch for your business and let them know you'll be available for questions after the presentation.

10. Send the event coordinator a thank you note!

For additional value, have a product available for sale at the back of the room such as a book, workbook, or audio recording. Most organizations are happy to provide you with a display table and the ability to promote your products and services. You can also provide the audience with a special offer. For example, "Save 30% off a consultation when you schedule with me today!"

You might be surprised by how quickly your business can grow as a result of your speaking engagements. Soon, you may find that you don't have to go looking for speaking opportunities. As you build a reputation, the invitations to speak will come to you. And after you do enough free speaking, you will inevitably find opportunities for paid speaking engagements. These can range from a stipend of $50 up to thousands of dollars. Professional keynote speakers earn from $3,000 to $10,000 and up for presentations and also have all travel expenses paid.

How to Find Speaking Opportunities

Contact local chambers of commerce and service groups such as Rotary and Kiwanis. For trade associations, search online for <your city> plus "association," "group," or "organization." Also, start letting peers and clients know that you're available to speak. Ask what groups they belong to and if they can connect you with the right people. It really isn't that hard to get booked once you start looking around.

Resources for Speakers

- ❖ www.toastmasters.org – Find a chapter near you to learn the craft of speaking professionally

- ❖ http://www.nsaspeaker.org/ — National Speakers' Association

- ❖ http://www.astd.org/ — American Society for Training and Development

- ❖ http://www.asla.com/ — American Seminar Leaders Association

- ❖ http://speakernetnews.com – Free newsletter with subscriber tips for speakers

LinkedIn Groups

- ❖ http://www.linkedin.com/groups?gid=48422 – ASTD National

- ❖ http://www.linkedin.com/groups?gid=125470 – Global Keynote Speakers Association

- ❖ http://www.linkedin.com/groups?gid=1742397 – Need a Speaker/Be a Speaker

- ❖ http://www.linkedin.com/groups?gid=37544 – Professional Speakers and Seminar Leaders

Books

- ❖ *Speak and Grow Rich* by Dottie Walters and Lilly Walters

- ❖ *The Wealthy Speaker* by Jane Atkinson

- ❖ *Money Talks: How to Make a Million as a Speaker* by Alan Weiss

In-Person Events

Yet another opportunity that puts you at the front of the room and allows you to demonstrate your authority is hosting your own events. These can include any of the following:

- ❖ Class or workshop
- ❖ "Lunch and Learn" session
- ❖ Open house or customer appreciation party
- ❖ Fundraiser for local charity
- ❖ Conference
- ❖ Weekend-long retreat
- ❖ Networking event
- ❖ Trade show or services showcase (held with peers)

Your events can be free or paid, and there are pros and cons on both sides. For free events, you may get more registrations than actual attendees. Because there is no personal investment, there can be less commitment to show up. For paid events, your audience may be smaller than it would be if it was free.

Any kind of event that you hold gives you a chance to reach out and invite your audience, plus get exposure with media and online event calendars. Perhaps you have some local prospects who have been circling around you but haven't quite been willing to make an investment. A free event might be just what you need to dazzle them and convert them into paid clients.

Event Promotion

Once you decide to hold an event, you need to spread the word as much as possible. Here are some suggestions:

- ❖ Promote your events on local community calendars. Your local newspapers, magazines, and news programs likely have free events calendars available and some may even write a brief article about your event.
- ❖ Create a free event listing with www.craigslist.org.

❖ Check out www.fullcalendar.com. For about $20 they will promote your event to dozens of publications in a metro area.

❖ Send an announcement out to your email subscribers.

❖ Promote the event via social media—repeatedly.

❖ Send a press release to local media.

❖ Remind people about the event. People often wait until the last minute to register, so repeat exposure is golden here.

❖ Ask peers and clients to help you spread the word.

❖ Attend local business networking events and hand out fliers.

❖ To manage the event registration process, try www.eventbrite.com.

Lead a Group

In 2006, I launched the Sacramento Speakers Network with five people at a local Starbucks. Today, we have the largest business network on Meetup in the Sacramento area and pack the house at our monthly meeting. The truth is that I call this group a "happy accident." My sole intention when it started was to network with other speakers in the area. But over the years, leading the group has brought me clients, speaking invitations, media interviews, corporate sponsorships, and tremendous visibility with the local business community.

I run my group with www.meetup.com, a fabulous tool for organizing local groups and events. In any given city, you can find a wide variety of options from business-related groups, singles groups, hiking clubs, religious organizations, political interest groups, book clubs, and much, much more.

Consider how leading a group could help establish you as an authority in your own community. Even if you operate a global business, you will find many benefits when connecting with clients in your own backyard. Here are some ideas:

❖ A business consultant who works with nonprofits could start a business group for nonprofit leaders.

❖ A career coach could start a group for job seekers.

❖ A professional organizer could start a group for the "chronically messy."

❖ A nutritionist could start a healthy living group.

❖ An executive coach could start a C-level business community.

How to Start Your Own Group

1. **Meeting Focus** – Do your homework to find out what other groups are already active in your community so you can make sure yours has a unique focus. For my speakers group, we focus on the business of speaking—which sets us apart from Toastmasters, where members practice their presentation skills. There were also no other speaking-related groups in the area, so this made it easy for us to stand out.

2. **Meeting Format** – Create a formal agenda that is fun and interactive. For my group, every attendee gets to give a 30-second introduction, which they love because you learn about who is in the room and also get to promote your services. It's interesting and fun (thanks to a lot of humor in the room) and sets the tone for the meeting. We feature a guest speaker with Q&A for 30 minutes, then end with a unique "mastermind" feature. Here we draw business cards, and selected attendees get five minutes in the spotlight to share a business issue or challenge and get feedback from the group. This is an extremely popular feature of the meeting. Figure out what would motivate your attendees and build that into your plan. Also stick to your agenda. Attendees appreciate it when you respect their time and run the meeting in a professional way.

3. **Relevant Guest Speakers** – If it makes sense, invite guest speakers to contribute each month. We've had a literary agent, several professional keynoters who have shared insights on the industry, book writing coaches, web technology discussions, and more.

4. **Raffle** – Another feature that makes our meeting fun is the raffle at the end of the meeting. Attendees are invited to donate

prizes, which can include books, audio programs, videos, workbooks, gift certificates for their services, etc. We draw business cards and winners come up to pick a prize. This is a lot of fun for all, and prize contributors get some extra exposure for their participation.

5. **Consistency** – Holding the meeting at the same time and place each month makes it predictable and helps to encourage attendance.

6. **Location** – Because our group has grown in size over the years, we have outgrown numerous locations. You could start yours at a coffee shop or restaurant. If you have access to office space or a conference room, that can work great, too. We outgrew all of the smaller venues and now meet at a local hotel, which adds a nice level of professionalism to the group. Meeting space at local hotels can also be more affordable than you might think. Make some calls and get some quotes if this appeals to you.

7. **Money Matters** – You can offer your group for free or charge for admission. When we held our meeting at a restaurant, the cost of admission was the price of dinner. Because we now rent space at a hotel, we charge $10 for attendees who pre-pay online or $15 at the door. I could certainly charge more, but I choose to keep meeting fees low to encourage growth. Your meetings could certainly become a revenue stream for you as well, though weigh that concern with the future potential for new clients and community visibility. I personally would rather my meetings be well-attended than worry about earning revenue from them.

Because of the size of our group and its focus, we've had several corporate sponsors over the years. This is a nice perk that provides added funding for the group. Meetup.com actually brings sponsor offers to large groups, though you can certainly pursue your own sponsors as well.

8. **Group Organization** – I honestly spend very little time managing my group each month. I book speakers months in advance and only need to update meeting details on the website and send out reminder messages. However, it does help to have volunteers to help collect money at the event, greet people as they arrive, time the introductions and speakers, and handle other relevant details.

9. **Group Promotion** – Meetup will automatically promote your group to existing members of the site, which is a huge advantage. Of course, you will also want to announce it to your networks and begin to get the word out. I send reminders out on social media, but that's about where it ends.

The truth is that I have never made much effort to advertise my group. It's not on my business card and it's admittedly not something I spend much time promoting. The members are loyal and tell their friends. Word of mouth is incredibly helpful in building your membership, so be sure to simply ask your members to spread the word. I constantly hear things like, "Three different people told me about the group and I finally decided to check it out!"

Business Networking

Early on in my entrepreneurial life, I hopped on the business networking train and enjoyed the ride. I joined several local groups and got to know many wonderful people in my community. But eventually, I hit a wall and burned out on the whole scene.

While I still believe that there is value in belonging to certain organizations for a period of time, often these groups have a limited life span. Once you know everyone there is to know and you realize you aren't generating much business as a result, it may be time to move on.

Another factor that drove me crazy was the whole concept of meeting for coffee or lunch for one-on-one time. The mere fact that we exchanged business cards and rubbed elbows at an event led to some unwritten rule that we should now spend an hour together—even if our businesses couldn't be further apart on the spectrum. To me, this became a gigantic waste of time, and too much interruption to my schedule.

What also happens as you build more of an audience online is that your local networks no longer hold all of the power. My business quickly shifted to a model where at least 70% came from online sources. Though I will always want to be involved in my community, it became clear that my time was better spent with online efforts and far fewer local networking meetings.

With that said, I still believe there is a lot of value in business networking groups. There are also certain businesses that need that extra personal touch and do well here, including life coaches, insurance agents, mortgage brokers, financial advisors, and anyone who offers services specifically for the local community.

There are certainly benefits to knowing people in your community, even if the only benefit you can identify is that it got you out of your home office cave and forced you to wear a nice pair of pants! But seriously, there is power in making human connections, and being an entrepreneur can be a lonely business. So if your only motivation is to get out and be with people, that is totally fine, too.

But if you're involved in any networking groups, I would like to encourage you to analyze the benefits you are receiving. As entrepreneurs, we have a limited number of hours in a day. When you treat your time like money, you can make decisions to spend it more wisely. You may think that all that networking you're doing is bringing you new business, but when you look more closely you may find that two of your three networking groups aren't producing results. You can't know what's working if you aren't tracking the results.

Analyzing Your Customer Data

To gain a better understanding of your clients and where they've come from, make a list of all of your clients from the last two years. I recommend doing this in a spreadsheet so that you can keep a running record to review periodically.

Next to each client name, write in the amount of revenue earned (note that you may be able to export this information from your accounting software depending on how you keep your books). Then, sort the list based on your highest revenue-generating clients to your lowest. Lastly, next to each client note how they found out about your business. Did you meet at a networking event? Were they referred to you by someone? Do they follow you on Twitter? Did they respond to a direct mail campaign? Be as specific as possible to get a good grasp on how they found your business.

Once you finish your list you should have a clear picture of how clients come to your business. More importantly, you will have a road-map of the strategies that have proven effective in generating business so that you can *do more of what has worked for you.*

You may find that certain people are referring the majority of business your way. If that's the case, be sure to cultivate those relationships and appreciate those people. If specific ad campaigns bring you business, then consider whether you should do more advertising. If your costs to place ads are less than the new revenues generated as a result, then increasing your advertising spending makes sense.

By the same token, if there are marketing campaigns you've run that haven't made an impact on client acquisition, then avoid repeating those mistakes. I recently asked a colleague how many clients she had landed as a result of her weekly networking group. She told me that the year prior she acquired three new clients, but this year she hadn't signed any. We determined that she was wasting 16 to 20 hours per month in a group that wasn't generating results. Her time could be much better spent on other revenue-generating activities.

If for some reason you're unable to capture client data from recent years, start now. Ask every new client how they heard about you, and train your staff to do the same. Document sales figures, and soon you will begin to see trends. The goal should always be to do more of what works and to let go of any marketing strategies that aren't producing results.

Also remember our earlier discussion in Chapter Three on strategic networking and referrals. It might be more beneficial to join industry-specific trade associations and related groups to reach either the people who can refer more business to you or the specific audience members you want to reach.

Direct Mail

Despite what you may think, direct mail and other traditional marketing methods are not dead. In fact, direct mail may be more relevant than ever because fewer companies are using this method, making it easier for those who do to stand out.

Another benefit of direct mail is the repeat exposure it can bring. Remember that prospects usually need to be exposed to a product six to eight times before they buy. When you reach out with a mail campaign, you've checked one of those exposures off the list! From sales letters and fliers to product samples and postcards, getting attention from inside a mailbox is easier and more affordable than ever. Inexpensive printing services like http://vistaprint.com, http://nextdayflyers.com, and http://iprint.com make it easy to create targeted campaigns.

Why Postcards Make Great Marketing Collateral

When it comes to traditional marketing tactics and direct mail, postcards remain my favorite type of marketing collateral for a bunch of reasons. For starters, they are relatively inexpensive to print and mail. Also, since a small percentage of direct mail is actually opened by recipients, postcards greatly increase your chances of getting people to notice because they stand out in a sea of envelopes. I also favor oversized postcards (8.5 x 5.5) because these *really* stand out.

Here are some of the ways I use postcards for marketing:

Individual Products and Services — When I launch a new product or service, I usually have a postcard designed. I either rent a mailing list (from a source like InfoUSA.com) and/or send out to my internal mailing list.

Package Inserts — Postcards make great inserts in packages that are mailed out. I like to write a personal note on the back of a postcard when sending something along to a client or a prospect.

Conferences and Events — Postcards also work well on display tables at conferences and events. They are more substantial than a flier and usually have more aesthetic appeal (especially the oversized version).

Bag Stuffers — Recently, I was invited to submit 500 fliers for stuffing in conference bags and instead, I decided to use postcards. In lieu of a purely promotional postcard, I printed up a list of tips for the audience on the front of the card and saved the promotional messaging for the back of the card. My goal was to provide something that attendees might keep or even post next to their desks. In a folder full of basic fliers, my postcard really stood out.

Personal Stationery — There are plenty of places to buy standard business stationery, but for years I have used custom postcards instead of boring note cards. I purchase high-quality photo art from iStockphoto.com and place a favorite motivational quote across the image. On the back side, I simply include my contact information at the bottom and leave plenty of room for writing a note. Though I love technology and use it every day, I still cherish a handwritten note and try to write them as often as possible.

Publish a Book

I cannot imagine what my career would look like if I hadn't authored books. Hands down my books have brought me more opportunities, credibility, and exposure than anything else I've ever done. If you want to be considered an authority in your field, then writing a book is your best ticket to get to where you want to go. Following are some of the many ways a book can help you build your business.

1. **Impress Prospects** — Meeting with a potential client? Bring along a copy of your book. Being an author elevates your credibility, demonstrates your authority in your field, and creates a competitive advantage.

2. **Attract New Business** — Want to land a meeting with a hard-to-reach prospect? Send him/her a copy of your book along with a personal note. The results may surprise you.

3. **Raise Your Rates** — Because your author status can equate to new clients, media coverage, speaking engagements, and a lot more, it can be easy to justify an increase in your rates.

4. **Generate Referrals** — I know a family law attorney who sent copies of her parenting book out to marriage therapists all over town. Since therapists were often talking to her potential clients—people going through divorce—she took a chance that the book might make an impression. Her practice quickly became the largest of its kind in her city. Introduce your book to people who are influential in your industry.

5. **Attract Media Coverage** — Media professionals are in constant pursuit of experts for stories and as an author, you have tremendous value to offer. A book makes you a credible source for interviews.

6. **Dazzle at Trade Shows** — When you host a booth at trade shows, your booth won't be ordinary once you showcase your book. Prospects and potential alliance partners will be eager to meet the author, especially if you are available to autograph books. Talk about a great way to stand out among the vendors!

7. **Develop New Profitable Programs** — Whether you ask them to or not, readers will call, write, and send email inquiring about how to implement the strategies in your book. Consider developing coaching programs, training packages, workbooks, and information products that complement your book.

8. **Conduct Speaking Engagements** — Authors are often invited to speak at trade association meetings, local chambers of commerce, nonprofit organizations, corporate functions, conferences, and events. A book makes you an obvious choice as a speaker. One of my clients, Donna Hartley, a professional speaker by trade, said that after her books were released (*Fire Up Your Life* and *Fire Up Your Intuition*), she was booking more speaking business as a result.

9. **Sell Large Quantities** — Could a trade association purchase and give away copies of your book to new members? Could a corporation use your books for training materials? Would your book provide inspiration for a local nonprofit group? Could your local bank offer your book as a bonus for those

opening new business accounts? Offer deep discounts on bulk orders and create a win-win situation.

How to Develop an Interesting Book Concept

There are many ways to develop a compelling book that will capture the attention of your target audience and accomplish your goals. Here are some options to consider:

- ❖ Reveal details about your company history
- ❖ Share compelling customer case studies
- ❖ Tackle an important issue in your industry
- ❖ Provide methods for using your products and services effectively
- ❖ Hold a contest to collect story submissions (and generate media exposure from the start!)
- ❖ Feature the story of a company executive (or multiple executives)
- ❖ Create a workbook for use with your products or services
- ❖ Sponsor a charity by developing a book that they can use for promotion or as a profit center
- ❖ Compile articles, essays, personal stories, case studies, materials from strategic partners, or any other content that can be assembled into a great anthology-style book

How to Write a Book: Eight Easy Steps to Get It Done Quickly!

Studies show that up to 80% of people have considered writing a book. And while this may sound like a major undertaking, it just might be easier than you think. Following are eight simple steps to finally get your book written in as few as 60 days (really!).

1. **Decide on a Topic** — Start by identifying your target audience. Whom do you want your book to reach? Are you writing for your clients, single mothers, consultants, teenagers, retired baby boomers? Knowing your audience will help you make important decisions when building your content. You should always keep your audience in mind as you develop your book.

2. **Know Your Book's Unique Value** — There were more than 500,000 book titles published in 2010 alone, so if you're worried that there is not enough room in the world for another book, know that the marketplace will always welcome new titles. The key is to establish how your book will be *different or better than the competition.*

    Determine what unique value you bring to your readers. Also important is your purpose for writing the book. If your book is a tool for promoting your business, the amount of competition will be far less relevant. But if you aspire to hit the best-seller lists, then it is essential to know the competition and be able to differentiate it from the rest.

3. **Choose Your Process** — You don't have to be a professionally trained writer to develop a book. Here are several alternatives:

    ❖ Hire a ghostwriter

    ❖ Enlist a co-author

    ❖ Dictate your book using software such as Dragon Naturally Speaking to convert it to text or have recordings transcribed and edited

    ❖ Get your thoughts on paper and hire a good editor to turn it into a manuscript

    ❖ Assemble an anthology of contributions from others

4. **Leverage Content You Already Have** — Your book may already be further along than you realize. If you have created content for your business, you may be able to use it for your book. Here are some places to look:

    ❖ Articles and blog posts you have written

    ❖ Handouts you have developed

    ❖ Surveys you have conducted

    ❖ Case studies, white papers, and client success stories

    ❖ Seminars, videos, and recordings that can be transcribed

❖ Contributions from others (articles, interviews, case studies, etc.—with their permission, of course)

5. **Get Started with an Outline** — Everyone has their own unique process for writing, though most writers will tell you that they start with some sort of outline. I recommend using the storyboard process.

   Start with a blank wall and a stack of Post-it notes or a pack of 3x5 cards. Write each and every topic idea, no matter how large or small. Once you have all of your ideas out, move the notes around until they form some kind of logical order. This is a great way to identify your chapters, how much content you have for each, and where you need to add more content. You can transfer everything to an outline or simply work off of your wall of ideas. This book was written using this process!

6. **Begin the Writing Process** — Once you know what topics to cover, you are ready to begin writing. The idea of writing a book can seem overwhelming, but if you tackle it in small pieces, it can come together quickly. Here are some ways to manage the writing process:

   ❖ Approach each topic as if you were writing a short article. This will help you stay focused on the topic at hand while making it easy for your readers to enjoy.

   ❖ Break up the text with plenty of sub-headings and bullets for easier reading.

   ❖ Share stories (real-world or fiction examples) and use metaphors to illustrate important points.

   ❖ If you get stuck on a topic, move on to something else and return to it later.

   ❖ Avoid editing while you write—this can slow you down. Write first and edit later.

   ❖ Beware of getting sidetracked. If you stop the writing process to research something online, it can be easy to lose track of time. Make a note about the added work you need to do and keep writing.

❖ Develop a system for jotting down notes when you need to add more information, look up a resource, or any other kind of follow-up. You might mark a spot in the manuscript with "xxx" so that you can easily search and follow up later.

❖ Include quotes from people you have interviewed, provide resources for additional information, and compile brief sidebar tips to enhance the reader's experience.

❖ Don't obsess about the length of your manuscript as it could affect the quality of the content you write. Focus on writing for the reader and getting the most important points across. If you need to expand your manuscript later, you can always add case studies, sidebars, statistics, or other data.

7. **Make Time to Write** — One of the biggest excuses that aspiring authors have is a lack of time to get a book written. Like anything else in life, if you want it badly enough, you have to find a way to make it happen.

You may want to plan your writing time around when you are most creative. Are you a morning person or a night owl? Perhaps you need to get up an hour earlier or stay up an hour later. It is important to discover your own unique process. Some writers are disciplined and write during a set time each day. Some schedule one or two days each week for writing. With my busy schedule, I actually check in to a hotel for a weekend and write! It's all about what works best for you.

8. **Cross the Finish Line** — The average book manuscript is around 60,000 words. Two typed pages are the equivalent of around 1,000 words. So if you wrote just two pages per day, your book would be done in 60 days! And as mentioned previously, manuscript length is not a deal-breaker, especially when publishing a book yourself. If yours comes in shorter

than average, a good book designer can still create an effective finished project.

Once your manuscript is complete, you will begin the editing process. Editing is essential to every book as typos and other errors can be distracting to the reader. A good editor can clean up basic grammar and punctuation issues or provide a more in-depth examination of your manuscript and suggest improvements.

Writing a book is a big achievement and can have a tremendous impact on your business. Set a goal to finally write that book this year and you will embark on a fantastic journey.

Publish an Ebook

Ebooks have been exploding in recent years. In 2011, Amazon announced that Kindle books were outselling all books on the site. Astounding! To take advantage of this huge growth curve, authors should convert printed books into ebooks.

To get on the ebook gravy train, set up an Amazon Digital Text Platform account (http://dtp.amazon.com) and distribute a Kindle version of your book. Also, submit your manuscript to http://smashwords. com. This handy service will convert your work into nine different ebook formats and make them available to Barnes and Noble Nook, iPhone and iPad, and many other outlets. With the combination of Amazon and Smashwords, you can cover the major ebook outlets, have immediate access to sales statistics, while reaching a growing network of readers.

Also note that if you're going to write a book or an ebook, in most cases you should make it available in both formats: print and ebook. The reading market is still divided and will be for some time. Don't miss out on readers by simply publishing one or the other—produce both!

As a writer, publisher, and avid book lover, I wrote an entire book on this topic: *Booked Up! How to Write, Publish, and Promote a Book to Grow Your Business*. You can also find lots of resources and information on the blog at http://AuthorityPublishing.com.

Corporate Sponsorships

The perfect topic to conclude this book is a discussion on corporate sponsorships. When you follow the strategies listed throughout this book, establish your authority, build a solid web presence, cultivate your audience, and become a leader in your niche, this culmination can lead to lucrative corporate sponsorship contracts.

All kinds of big companies look to experts for support. I have been involved in numerous corporate sponsorships over the years, and they have resulted in significant revenues and even greater audience exposure.

Here are some types of corporate sponsorship opportunities.

Paid Blogging – More and more companies are turning to experts and authors to generate content for their blogs and websites. Pay rates vary, but can range from $.50 to $2 per word. In many cases, you can generate ongoing contractual agreements to write for a company blog one or more times each month, creating a consistent revenue stream.

Sponsored Blog Posts – Get paid to write a blog post and mention the company or a specific product or service. There is nothing shady going on here, since part of the agreement should include full disclosure to your readers to conform with FTC guidelines for advertising online.

Blog Syndication – Some companies want to feature great content on their websites by syndicating content from existing blogs. If you're approached about syndicating your content on a major company website, know that this can bring valuable exposure for you. These types of arrangements are rarely paid, though the exposure usually makes them worthwhile.

Licensed Content – If you have an ebook, special report, or similar content, you can license the rights for a company to distribute your materials. Licensing agreements typically include a fee for a specified number of copies. Best of all, licensing digital content will cost you nothing and can be a purely profitable venture. For example, if your ebook covers sales strategies, a corporation that markets to sales people can purchase the rights to give copies away on its website or at live events.

Books – If you have authored a book, you can sell it in bulk to corporations to distribute at their conferences and events.

Some will pay extra to have their logo printed on the cover or special content added to the interior.

Sponsored Tweets – More and more companies are turning to experts who have large followings on Twitter and offering to pay for individual tweets or setting agreements to help sponsor a contest or event.

Webinars – You can get hired to deliver webinars on behalf of a company to their audience or as sponsored by the company to your own audience. This could be a one-time opportunity or delivered as a series over a period of time.

Spokesperson – Similar to how the major makeup manufacturers hire models to represent their brands, you can get hired as a spokesperson for a company initiative. Responsibilities can include conducting media interviews, working directly with a selection of the sponsor's clients, or speaking at events. Some will even hire you for speaking tours in multiple cities. Contracts like these are quite lucrative since you can typically negotiate a hearty retainer fee.

How to Get Corporate Sponsors

Simply implementing many of the strategies listed in this book can attract corporate sponsorships directly to you. When you stand out in your field, have a high-traffic website, a popular book, or a large social media following, I can assure you that you will be noticed. I have been involved in more than a dozen corporate relationships that have all come directly to me. This stuff works!

But you can also pursue relationships directly. The real key is finding companies that want to reach the same audience as you, and then offer them options for working together.

For example, if you're a fitness expert, you can pursue relationships with companies that manufacture fitness equipment and diet products, or offer related services. If you're an expert in productivity, you can market yourself to office supply companies, household organization suppliers, closet manufacturers, or companies that want to deliver productivity training to their clients or employees.

Start researching companies that would be a good match for you. A great place to look is in industry magazines and websites. If a company is spending money on advertising to your target audience, they may be interested in new marketing opportunities.

Finding the right contacts can involve some investigative strategies. I have used LinkedIn to locate some key contacts. For example, if you discover that a large company has a strategic initiative or even a special website devoted to reaching their audience, use the advanced search functionality on LinkedIn with keywords related to that initiative. I'm constantly amazed at how easy it is to locate those in charge of these things since they list the details in their profiles.

To contact them via LinkedIn, you will need to either get introduced by a mutual connection or pay to upgrade your account to allow you to send mail to contacts outside of your network. This small investment can pay off big time.

Here's another trick. Once you find a name for a contact, search for that contact on Google. Many times, you can easily find a direct email address.

Next, you will need to craft a pitch. There are about a million ways to approach this. Here is the formula I recommend:

1. Briefly introduce yourself and state your authority in your field. This means mentioning your credentials such as books you have authored, web communities you host, the large size of your social media network, etc.

2. Mention a specific initiative the company has or that your contact is responsible for. Let the contact know you are familiar with it and that you have ideas for how you could contribute.

3. Suggest a few options that you think would be a good fit, such as contributing to their blog, speaking at an upcoming event, or promoting to your audience.

4. Keep your communication brief, succinct, and professional. Hopefully, you will have the opportunity to expand on ideas and details later.

5. Close with a question like, "Can we schedule a brief phone call to chat about possibilities?" This can help ensure you get a response, and one that leads to the next steps.

Be patient with this process and expect that it won't be easy. Also, expand your search and focus on more than one company. I recently sent a pitch to a large company and didn't receive any response initially. A month later, I was contacted by the person I had reached out to with an entirely different opportunity than I had suggested. It worked out great and was well worth the small amount of effort involved in sending the pitch!

Final Thoughts on Owning Your Niche

I've outlined a lot of tactics here for you, including more than 175 links to resources. I would be surprised if you weren't overwhelmed by this information! And I know it sounds like a lot of work, and I'll be honest—it is. But many of these initial tactics will set you up for long-term rewards, and if you're like me, you may even find that you really enjoy the work required.

I feel fortunate that I get to write blog posts and content every day. It is incredibly rewarding to hear from readers and social media followers and know that my efforts have made even a small difference. I also have assistants who help with a lot of the tedious work, which gives me more time to focus on what I do best. Help from an assistant—or an intern—can be a smart investment.

My advice to you is to embrace these opportunities to raise your visibility online. It will take some time, but with consistent effort it will all start to pay off. Have fun, be yourself, and connect with your audience. Then, drop me a note and let me know how it's all working for you or how you liked this book. I love to hear from readers: Own YourNiche@BusinessInfoGuide.com.

Thank you for taking this ride with me. I wish you much success on your journey!

Quick Tip

Keep several versions (short, medium, and long) of your bio handy in a document that you can access at any time. This makes it easy to copy and paste into websites and articles, etc., whenever the opportunity arises.

Directory of Resources

If you would like a printable version of this directory of resources, you can download it here: http://businessinfoguide.com/reader-bonus/.

Marketing and Publicity

Help a Reporter provides free email alerts with media opportunities: www.helpareporter.com/

Survey Monkey conducts online surveys: www.surveymonkey.com

Craigslist offers free classified ads: http://craigslist.org

Internet radio shows and podcasts lists: http://authoritypublishing.com/store/internet-radio-shows-and-podcasts-lists/

Traditional media lists (radio, TV, print) and press release distribution:

http://authoritypublishing.com/store/media-lists-and-press-release-distribution/

Press release distribution: http://prweb.com, http://businesswire.com, http://prnewswire.com

Profnet is a paid online community of professionals available for media interviews: http://profnet.com

Technology Tools

Google's free keyword tool: https://adwords.google.com/select/KeywordToolExternal

Historical data from Google on keyword popularity: http://trends.google.com

Google search trends by location, category, product, or seasonality: http://google.com/insights/search

Free software downloads: http://download.cnet.com

Free modifiable organization chart template from Microsoft: http://office.microsoft.com/en-us/templates/TC060889761033.aspx

Google Alerts: http://www.google.com/alerts

Google Analytics: http://analytics.google.com

Google reader for RSS feeds: http://google.com/reader

Slideshare, for promoting your Powerpoint presentations:
http://slideshare.com

Blogging Services

WordPress: www.wordpress.org

TypePad: www.typepad.com

Blogger: www.blogger.com

Feedburner for managing RSS feeds: www.feedburner.com

Website Hosting

Host Gator: http://hostgator.com

GoDaddy: http://godaddy.com

Network Solutions: http://networksolutions.com

Blog Directories

Blog Catalog: www.blogcatalog.com

Technorati: www.technorati.com

Bloggapedia: www.bloggapedia.com

My Blog Log: www.mybloglog.com

Networked Blogs: www.networkedblogs.com

Blog Carnival: www.blogcarnival.com

Blog Flux: www.blogflux.com

Blogarama: www.blogarama.com

Blog Explosion: www.blogexplosion.com

Blog Hub: www.bloghub.com

Globe of Blogs: www.globeofblogs.com

Blog Hop: www.bloghop.com

Affiliate Programs and Ad Revenue

Google AdSense: http://adsense.google.com

Clickbank: www.clickbank.com

Commission Junction: www.commissionjunction.com

Linkshare: www.linkshare.com

Amazon Associates: http://associates.amazon.com

PayDotCom: http://paydotcom.com

E-junkie: www.e-junkie.com

Kontera: http://kontera.com

Chitika: http://chitika.com

Ad Brite: http://adbrite.com

Double Click: http://doubleclick.com

Buy Sell Ads: http://buysellads.com

Café Press: www.cafepress.com

Zazzle: www.zazzle.com

Free and Paid Advertising

Google Places: http://google.com/places

Yelp: http://www.yelp.com/business

Superpages: http://superpages.com

Google Adwords: http://adwords.google.com

Yahoo: http://searchmarketing.yahoo.com/

Bing: http://advertising.microsoft.com/
   search-content-advertising

Ask: http://www.ask.com/products/display

AOL: http://advertising.aol.com/

E-commerce

Google Checkout: https://checkout.google.com/seller/

Amazon Payments: https://payments.amazon.com

E-junkie: http://e-junkie.com

1ShoppingCart: http://1shoppingcart.com

PayPal: http://paypal.com

Payloadz (for electronic downloads): http://payloadz.com

Yahoo! Merchant: http://smallbusiness.yahoo.com/merchant

Practice Pay Solutions: http://practicepaysolutions.com

Infusionsoft: www.infusionsoft.com

Social Networks, Groups, and Forums

Self Growth provides online visibility for coaches, trainers, etc.: www.selfgrowth.com

Ning allows you to create your own social network or join one: www.ning.com

Groupsite allows you to create your own online group: www.groupsite.com

Google groups: http://groups.google.com

Yahoo groups: http://groups.yahoo.com

Meetup features local in-person networking groups: www.meetup.com

Social Media Tools

TweetDeck: www.tweetdeck.com

HootSuite: www.hootsuite.com

Refollow: www.refollow.com

Onlywire: www.onlywire.com

Pay with a Tweet: www.paywithatweet.com

We Follow: www.wefollow.com

Twellow: www.twellow.com

Refollow: www.refollow.com

Tweet Old Posts plugin for Wordpress blogs: http://wordpress.org/extend/plugins/tweet-old-post/

Expert Visibility Sites and Q&A Forums

Focus: http://focus.com

Quora: http://quora.com

All Experts: http://allexperts.com

Ehow: http://ehow.com

About: http://about.com

E-Newsletters

Constant Contact: www.constantcontact.com

iContact: www.icontact.com

Mail Chimp: www.mailchimp.com

Aweber: www.aweber.com

Article Marketing

Idea Marketers: www.ideamarketers.com

Ezine Articles: www.ezinearticles.com

Digg: www.digg.com

Go Articles: www.goarticles.com

One Minute University: www.oneminuteu.com

Articles Base: www.articlesbase.com

Scribd: www.scribd.com

Bizsugar: www.bizsugar.com

Paid Content

Squidoo : www.squidoo.com

Hub Pages : www.hubpages.com

Associated Content : www.associatedcontent.com

Helium: www.helium.com

eHow: www.ehow.com

Love to Know: www.lovetoknow.com

Sponsored Reviews: www.sponsoredreviews.com

Doc Stoc: www.docstoc.com

Day Tipper: www.daytipper.com

Examiner: www.examiner.com

Flixya: www.flixya.com

Review Party: www.reviewparty.com

Blogger Party: www.bloggerparty.com

Xomba: www.xomba.com

Triond: www.triond.com

Blogvertise: www.blogvertise.com

Wisebread: www.wisebread.com

Wire Tap: www.wiretapmag.com

Review Me: www.reviewme.com

Smorty: www.smorty.com

Pay Per Post: www.payperpost.com

Publishing Books and Ebooks

Authority Publishing provides custom book publishing services: http://authoritypublishing.com

Amazon Kindle: http://dtp.amazon.com

Smashwords (ebook distribution): http://smashwords.com

Google Books: http://books.google.com

Book Baby: http://bookbaby.com

Video Sharing Sites

YouTube: http://youtube.com

Viddler: http://viddler.com

Vimeo: http://vimeo.com/

Internet Radio Sites

Blog Talk Radio: http://blogtalkradio.com

All Talk Radio: http://alltalkradio.com

WS Radio: http://wsradio.com

Women's Radio: http://womensradio.com

Global Talk Radio: http://globaltalkradio.com

Purchase a list of internet radio shows: http://businessinfoguide.com/podcast-and-radio-show-media-lists/

Outsourcing

International Virtual Assistants Association: www.ivaa.org

Assist University (virtual assistants): www.assistu.com

Elance (freelance designers, writers, web development, etc.): www.elance.com

Guru (freelancers, consultants, accounting, legal, and more): www.guru.com

Rent a Coder (computer programmers): www.rentacoder.com

Paychex (payroll service): www.paychex.com

Grasshopper (toll-free online phone service): www.grasshopper.com

99 Designs (graphic design services conducted by contest): www.99designs.com

Teleconference and Webinar Services

Free Conference: www.freeconference.com

Instant Teleseminar: www.instantteleseminar.com

WebEx: www.webex.com

GoToMeeting: www.gotomeeting.com

GoToWebinar: www.gotowebinar.com

Intercall: www.intercall.com

Audio Acrobat records audios by phone: www.audioacrobat.com

Event Promotion

Eventbrite provides event registration management: http://eventbrite.com

Seminar Announcer: www.seminarannouncer.com

Events.org (promote your events): www.events.org

Full Calendar offers paid event announcements to media in major metro areas: www.fullcalendar.com

Resources for Speakers

Toastmasters: www.toastmasters.org

National Speakers' Association: http://www.nsaspeaker.org/

American Society for Training and Development: http://www.astd.org/

American Seminar Leaders Association: http://www.asla.com/

Free newsletter for speakers: http://speakernetnews.com

Printing and Direct Mail Services

Next Day Flyers: www.nextdayflyers.com

Vista Print: www.vistaprint.com

iPrint: www.iprint.com

Info USA sells mailing lists: www.infousa.com

iStock Photo provides high quality photos and images for purchase: www.istockphoto.com

Clipart offers royalty free images and photos by monthly subscription: www.clipart.com

Market Research

Monthly reports on a wide variety of consumer trends: http://trendwatching.com

User-generated online encyclopedia: http://wikipedia.org

A list of the most popular searches currently conducted on eBay: http://pulse.ebay.com

Consumer and business data with technology, IT, and marketing categories: http://forrester.com

Consumer census data by region including state, county, or city: http://quickfacts.census.gov/qfd/index.html

List of census data, including by industry: http://www.census.gov/epcd/www/guide.html

Sells mailing lists, though you can use its search functionality to get insight into the size of your target market: http://infoUSA.com

Database of market research reports (fee-based): http://www.marketresearch.com/

Market research data and a directory of certified research professionals so that you can find and hire help for conducting market research: http://www.marketingresearch.org/

Association of Strategic and Competitive Intelligence Professionals, where you can find firms to hire for assistance: http://www.scip.org/

Legal

The U.S. Department of Labor: http://www.dol.gov/

CAN-SPAM Act Details: http://www.ftc.gov/bcp/conline/pubs/buspubs/canspam.shtm

Corporate Direct (incorporate your business): http://corporatedirect.com

If you would like a printable version of this directory of resources, you can download it here: http://businessinfoguide.com/reader-bonus/.

About Stephanie Chandler

Stephanie Chandler is an author of several books, and is a frequent speaker at business events and on the radio. She has been featured in *Entrepreneur Magazine, BusinessWeek, Inc.com, Wired* magazine, and many other media outlets, and is a columnist for Forbes.com.

Stephanie is also founder and CEO of AuthorityPublishing.com, which specializes in custom publishing for nonfiction books, and BusinessInfoGuide.com, a directory of resources for entrepreneurs. She resides near Sacramento, California with her husband, son, a one-eyed cat, and a dog named Mojo (both rescue animals!).

Author/Speaker Details: StephanieChandler.com
Twitter: @bizauthor
Facebook: facebook.com/AuthorStephanieChandler
Email: OwnYourNiche@BusinessInfoGuide.com

Books by Stephanie Chandler:

LEAP! 101 Ways to Grow Your Business

From Entrepreneur to Infopreneur: Make Money with Books, eBooks and Information Products

Booked Up! How to Write, Publish, and Promote a Book to Grow Your Business

The Author's Guide to Building an Online Platform: Leveraging the Internet to Sell More Books

The Business Startup Checklist and Planning Guide: Seize Your Entrepreneurial Dreams!

The Conference Catcher: An Organized Journal for Capturing Ideas, Resources, and Action Items at Educational Conferences, Trade Shows, and Events

Own Your Niche: Hype-free Internet Marketing Tactics to Establish Authority in Your Field and Promote Your Service-Based Business

Need a Speaker?

Do you know of an organization that would benefit from a presentation based on topics from *Own Your Niche*? Stephanie Chandler travels from Sacramento, California and welcomes opportunities to speak at business conferences and events. Please email us with information: OwnYourNiche@BusinessInfoGuide.com.